What People

Bleedership is a realistic way to d
leading successfully in and throu
from the exceptional. No soldier wins a medal or gains notoriety of
valor in peacetime. It's only in times of war and conflict, yes crisis,
that exceptional bravery is needed and leadership is evidenced. My
friends, Dr. David Fletcher and Dr. Scott Barfoot, have coordinated
a wide array of real-life leaders leading in crisis. Others have bled as
leadership personifying bleedership. You will laugh, cry, get angry,
celebrate and often say "me too." No leader reading this book will be
disappointed.

Samuel R. Chand, DD
Leadership Consultant
Author

If you're a leader, crisis leadership is part of your job description.
There's no way to avoid it. We can't plan our way, pray our way, or
think our way around it. We have to work our way through it. In
Crisis Leadership, Scott Barfoot and David Fletcher share real-life
stories from frontline leaders—and, more importantly, they share the
important life and ministry lessons learned along the way.

Larry Osborne, DMin
Author and Pastor
North Coast Church

In leadership, it's a matter of when, not if, you will be confronted by
crises. Spiritual leaders are not immune from this critical challenge
of leadership. In fact, no one observes leadership more closely than
when performing under pressure. Yet this dynamic of leadership
is too often absent in the training of leaders who lead in spiritual
circles. Thank you, Scott and David, for this incredibly practical and
insightful look into the lives of leaders doing what leaders are called
on to do—crisis leadership.

Reggie McNeal, PhD
bestselling author and leadership coach
Missional Leadership Specialist, Leadership Network

Leadership is not always a cakewalk. Often it includes kicks in the gut. If you want good advice about the difficult backside of leadership in a variety of scenarios, this book is full of great wisdom and solid advice. Digest what is here. It can help you in and through a crisis.

Darrell Bock, PhD
Senior Research Professor, Dallas Theological Seminary
bestselling author

In this practical volume showcasing a professional, advanced degree in formal theological education, pastoral leaders will find common themes of crisis that impede or improve their leadership impact. Crises in marriage or ministry reveal leaders as those willing to learn and live out new learning. Dr. Scott Barfoot and Dr. David Fletcher who shepherd respective DMin programs at Dallas Seminary and India—I belong to both the institution and nation—here present growth options from the crisis-fires of the leadership crucible for multipurpose application. Read with pen in hand. When meeting external complexity, uncertainty and ambiguity with internal discouragement, unbelief and regret, you will find your notes immediately beneficial.

Ramesh Richard PhD, ThD
Professor, Dallas Theological Seminary
President, Ramesh Richard Evangelism and Church Health

Having spent sixty years in college and seminary teaching, pastoral ministry in churches and military chaplaincy, I agree with Jesus as quoted in Matthew 6:34, "Each day has enough trouble of its own" (NIV). Crisis is an adequate synonym for trouble. Dealing with crises saps personal and corporate time and energy. Crisis Leadership, authored and edited by Barfoot and Fletcher, takes us into the dust and mud of battlefield crisis struggles, focusing on solutions. I look forward to more such intensely practical books from these authors.

John W. Reed, PhD
Senior Professor, Emeritus; Director of DMin Studies, Emeritus,
Dallas Theological Seminary
Chaplain Lt. Col. USAF, Res. Retired
Associate Pastor, Lakeview Congregation, Dallas

Crisis
Leadership

Personal Accounts From Leaders Who Found Their Way And Thrived

D. Scott Barfoot
David R. Fletcher

XPastor
P R E S S
Austin, Texas

ISBN 978-0-9855559-1-7

Published by XPastor Press
Austin, Texas
www.XPPress.org

Printed in the United States of America.

Front cover artwork by Jason Fletcher.

DEDICATION

This collaborative work is dedicated to those global servant-leaders who, by the grace of God, are called to courageously lead like Jesus in the midst of crisis for the sake of gospel. "Very truly I tell you, unless a kernel of wheat falls to the ground and dies, it remains only a single seed. But if it dies, it produces many seeds." (John 12:24 NIV)

Scott Barfoot
David Fletcher

TABLE OF CONTENTS

INTRODUCTION

Chances are if you are reading these words there are three remarkable things true about you.

First, you are a leader. Not just any kind of leader, but a growing leader that recognizes and values the collective wisdom gleaned from those who have gone before you.

Second, you are a leader engaged on the front lines of ministry marred by conflict, complexity, ambiguity, and uncertainty. These are the four infamous horsemen of crisis. They invoke fear and defeat into even the bravest of soldiers.

Third, while you might not always feel like it, you are courageous. As the American actor John Wayne once said, "Courage is not the absence of fear. It is being scared to death and saddling up anyway."

You are a remarkable leader: one that is growing, engaged in the battle, and courageously leading through crisis.

As you journey through the pages of this book, you will discover that you are not alone. Other remarkable men and women, just like you, have been leading through crisis and they have the scars and victories to prove it.

You will find a wealth of treasured insight and personal real-life stories scattered throughout these pages from those who model the art of leading through crisis.

LEAD WELL, LEAVE WELL
In the Midst of Success, a Senior Pastor Resigns
Justin Beadles

My wife says I'm at my best in a crisis. She's watched me in lots of them.

There was the time I had to bury the young elder whose family watched him drown. The time I sat with those I loved as the husband confessed his infidelities. And the time I counseled the parents of the three-year-old girl accidentally killed by her daddy. My wife is right. On countless occasions I've steeled my resolve and stowed my emotions in order to serve those in the midst of crisis. For reasons unknown to me, I actually want the ball when calamity comes to the game of life.

This time was different. This time the crisis was my own. I was about to have lunch with Rick, the elder I affectionately called "Pretend Dad", and tell him I was resigning from ministry. He had no idea of what I was going to say and I had no confidence in how to say it.

A few bites into our meal, I took a deep breath, looked square in his eyes and borrowed a Doc Holliday line from *Tombstone*: "The time has come for us to redefine the nature of our relationship." He looked perplexed and, in one of only a few times in my life, I was desperately searching for words. I tried again. "Rick, I am resigning from ministry." He said what I expected: "You've been here eleven years, this is a growing church and the people love you. Why in the world would you resign?" My response was feeble but truthful: "I just can't do it anymore."

Yes, I left when they loved me. That was 2011. Today, the church I served remains healthy and continues to grow. It may seem odd, but I want to explore the idea of leading well by leaving well. I'll show you the parts done well and the parts where I blew it. Hopefully, my story benefits you when the time for your departure comes.

Leading well by leaving well requires one to begin ministry with the end in mind. You must have your departure in mind on the day of your arrival. Be not fooled. Your departure is coming and the latest it will be is your death. Even if you plan to spend the rest of your life in your current ministry, you don't know how long that will be, so plan for your exit.

Two scriptures bolster my point. Luke 14:28-29 says, "Suppose one of you wants to build a tower. Won't you first sit down and estimate the cost to see if you have enough money to complete it? For if you lay the foundation and are not able to finish it, everyone who sees it will ridicule you."

While speaking directly to evaluating the cost of following Jesus, this passage also illustrates the necessity of preparing well to produce the desired outcome. If your desired outcome is a healthy and vibrant church, then you must work for it to be such, even beyond your tenure. James 4:13-16 says, "Now listen, you who say, 'Today or tomorrow we will go to this or that city, spend a year there, carry on business and make money.' Why, you do not even know what will happen tomorrow. What is your life? You are a mist that appears for a little while and then vanishes. Instead, you ought to say, 'If it is the Lord's will, we will live and do this or that.' As it is, you boast in your arrogant schemes. All such boasting is evil."

Here the reader is warned about presuming life will go exactly as they planned. Too often we think our task is complete by simply saying, "If the Lord wills, I will be here the rest of my life." Instead we should say, "I want to be here as long as the Lord wills." Then we should answer the question: How can I build an environment that functions well without me? Leaving is the last thing you will do and it has the potential to impact your church in greater ways than many of your current efforts. Do you want the people to flourish or falter when you're gone? If you want them to flourish, and only a fool wouldn't, then lead them well by leaving them well.

Some may object to this thinking. They may claim that giving early attention to your departure is premature or keeps you from being totally devoted to your current job. However, those same objectors likely contribute to a retirement account, have a Will and are trying to raise their children to be independent adults. I submit that giving early attention to your departure demonstrates total devotion to your current job and provides for the future well-being of those entrusted to you.

The concept of leading well by leaving well was first brought home to me while I was serving in the U.S. Army. As a young soldier I was given the opportunity to lead a training mission to capture an enemy position. Eager to show myself capable to my superiors, I quickly took charge. I plotted the coordinates on the map, briefed the men and together we set off toward the objective. Midway through our trek we were on course, making good time, and I was feeling great about my leadership. Then the silence of the night was broken by the roar of gunfire. We'd been ambushed. Even though the bullets weren't real, few things get your blood pumping quite like having the enemy open up on you. My team reacted well and everyone survived, except me. For training purposes I was declared to have been blown to smithereens and the rest of the team was ordered to continue the mission. The leader replacing me was a good soldier who knew his job well. He consolidated his resources and reorganized his team only to discover that the only map to the objective had perished with me.

Had I taken the time to plan for my departure by ensuring that all had maps, the mission would not have been jeopardized. In language easily understandable, but far too coarse for this writing, it was communicated to me that I did not lead well because I did not leave well.

Having learned the hard way about leaving well, I determined to not repeat this mistake when I began work as a pastor. In my mind, avoiding this mistake meant instilling two core principles. The first, "Leadership will always be shared." And the second, "Succession will always be planned."

Sharing leadership didn't mean all decisions were made by a group or no one was in charge. It meant that I worked hard to establish a simple framework through which all employees and key volunteers could be empowered to make decisions, spend money and successfully conduct their ministries. Rather than create a policy manual explaining how and what each person should do, I chose to make a short list for each employee that outlined what they could not do. These short lists proved easy to monitor and provided the foundation for others to take ownership of their areas and share the leadership load.

As examples, the Finance Manager cannot fail to accurately account for all monies in accordance with generally accepted accounting principles. He cannot fail to provide timely and easily discernible reports on a regular or requested basis. He cannot fail to insure the property at 85% its replacement value at the best value and cost. This freed him to work according to a system of values as opposed to a set of instructions. The Worship Pastor cannot fail to choose songs whose words are true, are corporately singable and generate maximum congregational participation. If those three criteria were met, I didn't care what we sang. In both cases the personnel were guided by a set of values that enabled them to successfully minister without me.

Sharing leadership meant consistently ensuring the elders knew and fully embraced our priorities. At times this slowed the pace of needed progress, but their taking ownership of the church's priorities and structure was necessary for the mission to continue in my absence. Ultimately the successful sharing of leadership entailed me being able to successfully answer the question: Is everyone aware of and equipped to accomplish our objective?

On my first day in Nacogdoches, I started planning for my departure. I also planned to stay there the rest of my life. In the beginning, I never planned on or even considered leaving ministry. In fact, I viewed those who left ministry as either men who shouldn't have gotten in it to begin with or men who weren't very tough. Though neither large in stature nor fleet of foot, I would have placed my tenacity and toughness against any. I prided myself in my capacity to take a beating without whining or quitting. When I became the starting center on my high school football team while weighing 143 pounds, I could feel my father's approval.

My heart would swell with pride when my dad would recount to his friends my having broken a shoulder and silently embracing the pain—or the time I broke a leg while skiing and refused rescue from the Ski Patrol. He especially liked telling of my allowing an untrained army buddy to suture my face with no anesthesia.

I was proud, sinfully so, of my toughness. Ultimately, I believe it was this pride and one-sided toughness that led to my resignation from ministry in circumstances I never imagined. While resigning from ministry was painful, leaving poorly would have only made it worse. Forever will I be thankful for having structured an environment capable of flourishing without me. Reflection has shown me that there were at least five periods in ministry that contributed to my quitting. Unfortunately, I didn't see any of them coming. Perhaps my mistakes will preserve you from making them yours.

The Early Years

In the movie, *Black Hawk Down*, U.S. Army Rangers were tasked with rescuing crew members from two helicopters that had been shot down in the streets of Mogadishu, Somalia. Though well trained, these Rangers were untested in battle. When the bullets began to fly, one enlisted man shouted, "Colonel, they're shooting at us! Colonel, they're shooting at us!" The highly trained and battle-tested Colonel calmly replied, "Well, shoot back." The presence and clear direction of the Colonel kept his men from the paralysis that came from being initially overwhelmed.

My early years were emotionally a bit similar to the situation faced by the Rangers. In spite of good training, the nature and volume of crises stunned me. Within my first year I dealt with succeeding a pastor who had been asked to resign, fiscal mismanagement, a lawsuit and staff transitions. Through it all I maintained a steely-eyed exterior, but inside I was shell-shocked and at a loss as to how I should respond. In hindsight, I believe these first traumatic exposures added an unnoticed emotional weight that I should have better managed.

With the wisdom gained from failure, were I to repeat those early years, two things would be done differently. First, I would have stopped at nothing to gain frequent face-to-face access with a trusted and seasoned pastor. We would focus near exclusively upon the condition of my heart, the foundation of my fears and the faithfulness of Christ. In this relationship, the seasoned pastor must work hard to not simply trade war stories about ministry. The young guy must avoid just asking about the urgent: How do I preach better? Or, how do I best structure small groups? Second, I would have asked one or two of my most trusted fellow elders to periodically meet with this seasoned pastor and discover how we might best serve one another.

Through this arrangement, my fellow elders would have learned that I was afraid that they were listening to my sermons, all the time worried that I would say something inaccurate. Of course, I could have communicated this fear directly to the elders. Had I, this is what I would have heard: "No we're not." This would have been a true answer from them, but an incomplete address of my fear. Neither of us would have known where to go from there.

I can imagine the conversation between the seasoned pastor and my trusted elders.

"Guys, Justin is afraid you're worried he is going to make an inaccurate statement when he's preaching."

"No, we're not."

"I believe you, but tell me why you think he might be afraid."

"I don't know. Wait, the previous pastor made a few inaccurate interpretations and that caused us lots of grief. Come to think of it, we've probably told Justin more stories about the previous guy's failings than his successes."

"So, you guys are at least a little bit worried?"

"Well, maybe a little, but we love Justin."

"Try saying to Justin, 'We struggle with worry because of our past experience, but you've never given us cause to continue. In fact, we want you to know that if you make a mistake, it's not the end of the world. We'll work together and fix it.'"

"We can see how that would help." Had the previous conversation happened, it would have helped alleviate the fears of all involved.

Couples that have enjoyed a long and flourishing marriage realize that many fears and frustrations can be resolved by asking the right questions. Most will admit as newlyweds they didn't know what questions to ask. They learned how to more effectively solve their problems by forging a relationship with an older couple or seeking professional counsel.

In similar fashion, a young pastor typically doesn't know the right questions to ask to get to the root of his fears and frustrations. His fellow elders may have never given it much thought either. Bringing in a seasoned third party early prevents the buildup of frustration—and makes deep conversation about inevitable difficulties a normal part of ministry leadership.

The Weight of Success

Every pastor longs for things to go well; few can anticipate the added pressure this brings. In this church, new to me, things did go well, very well. Within the first three years, our church essentially doubled in size to approximately 600 people in attendance. We began having two services and still had to ask the young to sit on the floor during church. Regularly it was reported to me that my preaching was biblical, life-changing and enjoyable to listen to. All of this made me raise the bar on my performance every Sunday. In my opinion, attaining success is far easier than maintaining success. After initial success, the expectations of all are increased. Soon enough I found that the success I thought would make my life easier had actually multiplied my problems.

The success you desire may come, but not without a price. However, managing success is not altogether dissimilar to planning for your departure. In both cases, building an environment where people are enabled to flourish, learn from their failures, make decisions and function without you will enable the survival of success.

Unbalanced Toughness

Being tough is a good thing, but it can create a life subtly lived on the fringe of fatalism. My first response in difficulty was to simply tough it out. I typically looked at a situation and said, "That's the way it is, I'll just have to manage." Toughness is like a coin. On one side is the unflinching resolve to change circumstances. On the other side is the ability to steadfastly endure circumstances. Without realizing it, I lived like toughness was a one-sided coin. This unbalance led me to lose the sensibility to attempt to work out difficult situations and believe simple endurance was my only option.

Again, hindsight has revealed this pattern in dealing with difficulty was modeled to and developed within me from my earliest days. I had great parents who were faithful to Christ and both extraordinarily tough. My dad's concept of toughness enabled him to control or change his circumstances while my mom's was mostly observed in her ability to quietly endure. Both lived like the coin of toughness only had one side.

We lived on a farm, not close to anything. The trailer house I grew up in was clean but crumbling and inclement weather meant having to park at the entrance to the property and walking the remaining ¼ mile home. I know my mom wished for a well-built home and driveway, but she never complained. Instead of trying to change the situation, she resigned herself to it. Her silence was so complete it affected how others perceived her true wishes. If you had asked my dad how my mom felt about her living conditions, he would have said, "I guess she's happy … she never complains."

In this regard, I'm like my mother. Rather than voice frustrations, I'm learning that I tend to resign myself to them and I unconsciously expect the same response from others. My initial and sometimes only response of quiet endurance contributed to my resignation and complicated my relationships.

A good example came when I and my fellow elders embarked upon a building project. New space was necessary as the sanctuary was beyond capacity and the staff was stacked into an old house, now used as an office. Initially the plans called for a beautiful worship space along with an attached office complex for the team. However, when the price estimates returned, we all got nervous and decided to nix the office from the plan. It wasn't a fun decision. Nonetheless, we all believed it was the only option at the time.

The staff team and I moved from our old house into an older house and continued the work of ministry. It was a mess, but we didn't want to put much money into it as the hope was to construct an office on its location within a year or two. The church grew, the staff grew and the one year wait became seven. Early on, I unconsciously chose to demonstrate my toughness—not in pressing for provision, but by quietly enduring.

Honestly, it wasn't a huge issue for me and it certainly wasn't the cause of my resignation. Jesus didn't have an office and many pastors around the world don't either. I write this story only as an example of the fatalism that subtly crept into my heart. My response to this situation and many like it gradually increased my fatigue and negatively affected my leadership. If you had asked my fellow elders how I felt about the office, I imagine they would have said, "He's fine, he doesn't really care." And, if you had asked the same question of my staff, they likely would have said, "We need a better office, he doesn't push for it, so it seems like he doesn't care." The truth is; I personally didn't care much about the office. It would have been nice, but ultimately wasn't a big deal to me. The truth is also that I cared a great deal about getting my staff into a nicer and more productive work environment, but I assumed it would never happen, so I never brought it up.

Are you living like toughness is a coin with only one side? Doing so invites calamity and I am proof of such. If you choose only the side of pressing for change, you'll be seen as one concerned only with getting his way and unable to be pleased with anything. Choose the side of quiet endurance and people will assume you're content though you're frustrated and weak or uncaring because you don't press for change. Lasting success and joy in ministry is tied in part to a balanced expression of toughness. You must continue the belief that change is possible and press for it. And, you must simply endure, but not without hope.

The Regularity of Sunday

I like to preach and people other than my mother have said I'm good at it. I also like to run, though I've never been accused of being fast. Both are healthy enterprises that can break you if you're not careful. In either, the breakage is not sudden but subtle. Repetition of movement without adequate rest produces pain, amplifies fatigue and robs you of the joy of doing that which you love.

In addition to being tough, my parents were known for being incredibly hard workers. I can recall many times when my dad, brother and I would take shifts driving the tractor through the night and then going to school in the morning. It wasn't fun, but it was something we all took pride in. Nobody would ever associate the word "lazy" with the name "Beadles."

Though I began ministry with a determination to work hard,

I also determined not to do so at the neglect of my family. Thankfully, my wife would report that this balance was maintained. However, in spite of balancing the number of hours spent working, the regularity of Sunday began to take its toll. That which I loved began to be that which I dreaded. Perhaps dreaded is too strong of a word. It increasingly became more difficult to be energized by the prospect of preparing another sermon. Proverbs 25:16 illustrates my thought well: "If you find honey, eat just enough—too much of it, and you will vomit." You will loathe that which is delightful if you get too much of it.

To maintain health when running, you must drink before you're thirsty. So also, I now believe that health in preaching is maintained by resting before you're tired. From the beginning, and in addition to vacation, I should have scheduled one month per year with no preaching responsibilities. This would have allowed me to simply be at the church, attend the services and enjoy the worship. I considered it, but my fear of being thought as lazy kept me from implementing the plan. Among my decisions, I believe this was the dumbest.

From the beginning, plan a preaching schedule that works for you. Rest even if you don't feel tired—both you and your people will reap the benefit. A few will think you're lazy, but they probably already thought this before you decided to rest. No one that doesn't prepare and preach each week can appreciate the effort involved. It's not the hardest job in the world, but it's harder than it looks. So, rest for the sake of joy.

The Kid in the Room

People tend to relate to one another based upon the stage in life when the relationship blossomed. If you went to elementary school with someone who is now a physician, it's hard to picture him as such. Your memories of him playing dodgeball and pestering girls may cause you to prefer the opinion of a physician you only recently met—even if your classmate is the smarter of the two.

The youngest children of large families nearly always report being viewed by their siblings as perpetual children. While their relationships are genuine and congenial, they often don't believe themselves to be understood or that their thoughts are received equally among the others.

When you become a pastor in your twenties, you don't know much. More accurately, you know a whole lot about a very little. You know how to build a sword, but have yet to learn how to wield it. While you may have done a lot of things in life, you simply haven't lived enough of it. Your limitation is not lack of wisdom, it's lack of experience. Wisdom doesn't come automatically with time, but some wisdom does not come without it.

Thankfully, this truth was easy for me to embrace. My fellow elders were all considerably older than me. During the first years of ministry, I readily leaned heavily upon them for leadership and direction. I sought their counsel on decisions a more seasoned pastor would have made independently. Because this is how our relationship was formed, it became the lens through which we viewed one another, even after more than a decade together.

With respect, I say that it was hard for them to see me as anything other than the inexperienced 29-year-old guy they took a chance on. I say this of men that I loved and respected, men that loved me. I can assure you they meant me no harm. Conversely, it was hard for me to see them as anything other than men who wanted to be involved in the vast majority of all decisions. We inadvertently continued relating to one another on the terms in which our relationship began.

As children age, good parents actively change the lens through which they view them. While there will always be memories of adolescence, those memories are not allowed to diminish the independence that comes with adulthood. The changing of this lens is not automatic. It requires an active release to adulthood on the part of the parent and an active embracing of adulthood on the part of the child.

In the same manner, older elders and younger pastors must actively embrace modified views of one another as their relationship matures. In families, this modification works best when initiated by the parent. Taking the time to communicate with a child that you recognize is entering a new stage of life—and giving him the freedom and responsibility that comes with it—takes courage but results in a strong relationship and a healthy child. The best parents recognize the need to change the relationship before the child demands it. Doing so reduces relational friction and encourages the child to embrace the freedom and responsibility that come with age.

Ideally, older elders would initiate the necessary relationship changes as their young pastor ages, in both experience and years. They would communicate with him and the congregation the new authorities being entrusted. This both develops the maturity of the pastor and strengthens his relationship with the elders. When this relational modification happens, the pastor must humbly embrace this authority and increase the showing of his respect to those having given it to him. Romans 13:7 says, "Give to everyone what you owe them: If you owe taxes, pay taxes; if revenue, then revenue; if respect, then respect; if honor, than honor." Both the pastor and his fellow elders should frequently ask themselves two questions: "Am I increasingly demonstrating my respect in a manner easily received?" and, "Am I conducting myself in a manner worthy of respect?"

Leaving Well

As you can see, the mistakes I made at various stages in my tenure culminated in a man who prized his toughness having to admit he was at the end of his strength. I loved my fellow elders and the people, but I still believe if I hadn't mustered the strength to leave when I did, I would have missed the opportunity to leave well.

Had I not begun planning for my departure over a decade prior, I don't think I could have allowed myself to quit. Since we had worked hard to create an environment that could flourish beyond me, I could sleep well knowing the people entrusted to my care would not be left leaderless and naked to their enemies.

If you find yourself in a similar situation, perhaps answering the same questions I posed to myself prior to my resignation will be beneficial to you.

1. Is it realistic that I have the strength to continue as things are for the next 1-5 years? Every pastor will have days when he will say, "No." How you would answer the question over a period of several months or a year is more accurate.

2. **Can I realistically identify any key changes that could be implemented on a timetable that I can survive?** All of the difficulties I encountered were fixable, but I reached a point where the thought of trying to fix them, and the amount of time it would require, only increased my fatigue.

3. **Why don't I just get a job at a different church?** For me, the answer was simple. First, I didn't have the emotional energy to encounter the problems I was guaranteed to face at a new church. Second, the people at any new church would not be getting their best from me.

4. **Am I convinced that I've done all that I can to ensure the well-being of the congregation?** We had righteous elders and an excellent staff. In keeping with my value of always planning for departure, my fellow elders and I had invited our College Pastor to join our leadership team. At the time, I had no plans of leaving, but often said to my fellow elders, "If something happens to me, Kyle should be my replacement." Having him on the leadership team increased my assurance that the congregation would be well served without me.

On the evening following my lunch with Rick, we met as elders and I told them of my decision. Though disappointed, after hearing my explanation they blessed me as only ones who love you can: They allowed me to quit. Though at the time none of us understood the particulars, they were gracious to me when I was most in need of grace. I am forever in their debt. They're good men and worthy of respect. I left quietly and genuinely affirmed the leadership of the elders and excellence of the staff. The congregation honored my service beyond what I deserved.

Today, Kyle and another man serve as Lead Pastors, sharing the preaching load. Joy fills my heart, knowing the church continues to thrive. There are things I would do differently and many mistakes I wish I wouldn't have made. But, I believe ultimately that I led well when I left well.

IT CAN HAPPEN TO YOU
Being Served Divorce Papers While in Ministry
Tim Crow

We were young and in love.

We knew God wanted to work through us. We dreamed and prayed that He would use us for greater kingdom purposes. We were married on a hot July day in 1987, and two weeks later packed up our little U-Haul to begin life as seminarians. Seminary was a good fit, and we found newlywed bliss and seminary life "made for us."

There are few things I remember from my first semester in seminary—most of my memories had little to do with actual time in the classroom. Today, this is not a major admission, but for that time and place, education was the events that happened in the classroom. After all, the seminary assembled the best of the best in the area of theological and biblical studies. However, there was one lesson in one lecture that resonated with me.

During that first year, I was enrolled in the typical first year courses with well-known and respected teachers. The memorable learning came one day in the initial course in New Testament, a course that I was eager to take, with a professor I had heard great things about. As I sat in the course, I remember few things—very few things.

However, there was one day when the professor seemed to go "off script" from what seemingly had been given and perfected from a few decades of teaching. There was a day when I saw a bit of emotion from this beloved and respected New Testament professor. His baseline emotion had shifted slightly.

I remember that as he began the lecture, he reflected on students whom he had the privilege of teaching, who were seemingly finding "success" in ministry.

No doubt, there was a narrative known to him about one of his former students, who was in a greater public spotlight. Soon, he started to talk about infidelity in the life of the minister of the gospel. He had the attention of the classroom in a way that was previously not seen. It was obvious that a former student, who he deeply respected, had fallen into infidelity—and it was becoming known in the life of the church. That day, my professor looked at a fresh-faced group of seminarians and told us, "Remember, you are a person, and infidelity can happen to you as well. Do not think you are immune."

Of course, as a newlywed young man in my early twenties, I thought that this sage was a bit off about me: he was better at teaching Chronology than he was at discerning the future needs of young lovers. There was no way that I would ever be unfaithful to my beautiful wife.

The Petri Dish for a Crisis

The years after seminary were filled with life, adventure and fulfillment in ministry. My wife and I responded to the call to serve as missionaries, in the wake of the so-called fall of communism in Eastern Europe. We served and prospered in what many believed were harsh living environments, but life was good for us.

The primitive life had a pristine quality about it that resonated with our souls and calling. During this time, God was directing for me to begin a Ph.D. in England and life was moving in good fashion. I was teaching in a seminary, planting churches, and studying for a heady higher degree with a prominent mentor in the ancient Near Eastern world. However, after a decade of building a ministry in teaching and church ministries, it became clear that we were being directed back to the U.S. to take care of the needs of our family—nothing major, but necessary. Change was coming. I dreaded it. I had an unfinished Ph.D. I did not want to return to the U.S. Let me say it again: I really did not want to return to the U.S.

In many ways, my resistance to embrace God's direction for my life and ministry was the beginning of the "crisis." I felt very much out of synch in the U.S. My ministry had been torn away from me—in a word, I was discontent.

The discontentment sat on my shoulders, as an unwanted albatross, and began to fester, little to my knowledge. I was doing life in the church, serving in a church and adjuncting for a couple of Christian higher education institutes, but it simply was not "life on the mission field."

On top of the discontentment, I had an unfinished Ph.D. dissertation that seemed to nag me every day: a jilted lover. I made the decision that I needed to primarily invest myself in finishing the dissertation, so I resigned from the church. Even in this decision, there was discontentment that festered. I tried to pour myself into teaching and finishing my dissertation.

The Reality of the Sage's Words

Then it happened. In the late morning as I prepared for a lecture on the spiritual life, I received a knock on the door. I pulled myself from my desk to see who would be knocking in the early afternoon. As I peered out the window, I became unnerved at what I saw.

A huge truck was parked in the middle of my driveway, inches away from my garage door, with its engine running. And a seemingly even bigger man, who had the appearance of the baddest bouncer on earth, was standing in my driveway. As I walked out to greet him, he asked me a simple question: "Are you Tim Crow?" My mind raced as I wondered what he could possibly want. With my positive response, he said, "You have been served court papers."

My heart jumped out of my chest as I looked at a one-inch thick envelope. I was bewildered. What was this?

I was dumbfounded. Why would I be getting court papers? Surely a former student wasn't suing me? Mystified. As my mind raced, and my hands began to get the jitters, I opened the thickest envelope ever and read the first page: "If you do not respond in thirty days, then the court will proceed with a divorce." My heart jumped out of my chest as I tried to pull my thoughts together. In a blink my world was filled with questions. My wife was asking for a legal separation. My seminary professor was correct. My world had just been turned upside-down.

It's amazing how obtuse I was in the midst of the mounting storm of a crisis. The last thing I expected was the issuance of legal papers by my wife. In hindsight, I wonder how I could have been so naive to not think that this was a possibility.

The truth is we were going through a hard phase in our marriage. We had been working with a therapist to try to bring better health to our marriage. About once a month we would "take a stab" at standard therapy sessions. In truth, the therapy for me seemed like many fifty-minute blocks of wasted time over the course of a year. These sessions with the therapist were deeply frustrating for me. My theology was pervasive in my relational view: I am a sinner and I will offend. I will be offended. For me the answer was not to be found in a meeting with a therapist, but it was a radical commitment to the life and message of Jesus: forgive those who trespass against you.

My wife and I were two people who loved God and sought to live out our faith in good ways. Why would we need a therapist? I had decided that therapy simply was not working. The sessions stopped. I received the message. My wife decided that the marriage was not working.

Wisdom in the Immediate Hours?

In the hour after receiving the letter, I got a call from my wife. She had evidently been informed that the papers had been served. I called the pastoral leader of my church. How does a person go from receiving the news of separation or divorce and then transition to teaching a course on spirituality a few hours later? How does this happen? What was God trying to speak to me?

In the midst of a marital crisis, I was given the advice to call a pastor-lawyer friend of mine. I did. He told me that I needed to protect myself and retain a lawyer. The conversation then pursued a path discussing "how much lawyer" was needed to present my case. In a rather profane way, my friend gave me the name of a lawyer that would serve me, but not be top-notch due to my financial place in life.

Something struck me as odd, that the first recourse to a marital crisis was retaining the use of lawyers. After all, my wife and I were two people who loved God and sought to live His principles. What good was our faith if we walked a path of securing legal retainment for our issues? Was legal representation the first course of action that would be a healing course?

The Church Brokers a Deal: Part 1

In the days that followed, I tried to avoid allowing the shock turn into anger. In God's providence, the effect of receiving legal papers was an anesthetic as I sought help from peer-pastors. That brought my wife and me once again into the office of our pastor, who "negotiated" the deal: 1) removal of legal action on her part, and 2) commitment to marriage counseling on my part. With that, we started another period of marriage counseling.

We started having a weekly meeting with a third party, trying to help us sort through the issues in our marriage. For me, this was a weekly act in futility. I waited and wanted my wife to apologize for what I perceived to be her wrong action of taking legal actions for the health of our marriage. In many ways, that was all I wanted from her: an apology. In my view, she had been unfaithful by seeking the help of others—going through legal channels to bring change. Yet, the apology did not come. As the weeks and months progressed, a deep root of bitterness was forming as I waited for an apology. In hindsight I realize that I thought that the crisis was heightened by her clear actions—those actions were an attack on my reputation. The person who was supposed to protect me had instead brought harm to me. In the midst of the crisis, my concern was about my reputation and wounded pride. These issues were the stumbling block to any weekly therapy the best therapist could give.

As the weeks and months carried on, it was clear that therapy was not working. I watched as my wife's health started to falter; she was losing weight and her emotional well-being simply was dissipating. In those days, it was easy for me to see it, but my mind quickly rationalized that this was just as much her fault as mine. For me, the way out of the crisis was a path of her admission for her part of our marriage struggles.

After all, this is what marriage is: two people willing to meet each other in the middle. Culture had engraved on my mind that marriage was a 50/50 contractual arrangement, where score was often kept for the one not keeping his or her part of the contract. Our home was becoming extremely toxic to the point that many people in the community were now aware that "things were rocky in our marriage."

It all finally came to a head when I decided, in my righteousness, that the church had to make a firm stand and intercession for our marriage. If the church is the church, should it not have the ability to help couples in the midst of marital pain? I proceeded to write a letter asking our church to bring disciplinary charges against my wife for rumors that were being heard in our community.

Unknown to me, she was taking the same path. Our position in our local church gave our issues perhaps a more immediate attention. We were able to secure the pastoral help with an establishment of a group of leaders—to hear both sides and render a path of healing.

The Church Brokers a Deal: Part 2

The evening came for my wife and me to go to the church and make a case for our marriage, to help with a path of healing—which in my mind was placing the issue with my wife. The church had formed a group of leaders and individuals who would have insight into our marriage, serving as redemptive path-givers.

I vividly remember going into the meeting thinking how "solid" a case I had against my wife. My view was still on my pain and pride. After the initial niceties and background, I was given the opportunity to tell my narrative of the crisis in our marriage. After I was done, the one "outsider" to the group asked me if: 1) I trusted the church, and 2) if I would be obedient to the decision rendered by the group. On the inside, I was thinking, "You are wet behind your ears," as I swallowed and affirmed that I would honor the decision of the church.

I left the meeting while my wife entered the room to tell her story. I proceeded to go to the Wednesday evening prayer meeting. Yes, even with my marriage in crisis, I was going to the prayer meeting. Later that evening, the phone call came. My pastor-friend told me that in the morning I was to come to the church to hear their plan.

That morning, I went to the church and met with the "outsider." He handed me an envelope with the written outcome of the church: "We are recommending a period of separation with marriage counseling personally for both parties. We will support the idea of the husband being asked to leave the home as part of the process of healing."

I was dumbfounded. The church was asking me to leave my home. How could a church ask a father to leave the home? I heard the voice of the one outsider, "Will you be obedient to the decision of the group?"

Path to Healing: Six Steps that were Embraced

Living in an unhealthy marriage is hard on people. When I left the family home, I wish I could say that I had great remorse for the state of my marriage. I did not. Oh, I had remorse, but it was about not being with my children; it was the realization that people who had not known of the pain in my marriage would now know that my marriage had been unhealthy for years. As far as my thinking of marriage was concerned, there was a certain sense of release—that the end was near.

For a few days I had a sense of liberation: the crisis was over by the thought of a legal action to break a covenant made. Yet, God would soon intervene and reveal to me the need to renew my place in my marriage. Perhaps it was the crucible of pain and separation that brought the reality of my life into focus. Perhaps it was the prayers of the church that were working in a way that can only be a spiritual work on the behalf of a broken marriage. There are many mysteries that rest on God in the midst of the crisis. It was during this period that I embraced some steps that in the end were part of the process of healing.

1) Friends may be enemies in the marital crisis: They will take sides.
I found friends to be over-rated in the midst of a marital crisis. I realize in a culture saturated with the need for communities and support groups that this will receive some push-back, but the reality is that

friends are largely impotent as a means to help in marital difficulties. It became clear to me in the process that mutual friends will decide which party they are going to embrace. It quickly becomes like a game of middle-school kickball, with friends being divided onto two teams.

However, the danger is not the friends that land on the other team, but the ones seeded on the home-team. I soon found that "my friends" gave support to me in many unhealthy ways.

One day, soon into the separation, I realized that I needed friends who would have the courage to love me by pointing out my flaws.

However, on a cultural level this is contrary to the idea of "friend." A friend is one who accepts and loves—and is often blind—to those character traits that may have led a marriage down a toxic path. Early in my separation I made the "rule" that I would not allow negative speech about my wife to be part of the encouragement I would receive from friends.

2) Take the "high ground" and not retain a lawyer.

In a world and church culture that screams to protect yourself in the midst of a marital crisis, I went against the advice of friends. In and out of the church, when it comes to the "marriage crisis," there often is the default first step that most marriages facing separation and divorce embrace. Now don't get me wrong—there may be exceptional situations where you absolutely need to work with an attorney. Yet, I made the intentional decision not to retain a lawyer.

Like friends, lawyers have a key part that they contribute to the health of a marriage in trouble. Usually it is not to the healing of the marriage, but to a long process of breaking the covenant through legal channels. The very nature of "protecting myself" by retaining a lawyer seemed counterintuitive to me. As a child of God, I believed that God was the one who would protect me. The crisis of separation and divorce was a question of whether I could trust God to "protect me," rather than a self-interest lawyer and firm.

3) Understand that I was part of the crisis.

Self-examination is difficult, especially for those in the ministry. The ironic issue is that most people understand that there is a bundle of depravity "under the hood," waiting for a short-circuit, but there is a nagging desire to suppress this in the spiritual life.

It is axiomatic that blame was part of the aftermath of disobedience in Eden (Gen. 3), as the marital crisis whispers, "It is the other person's fault and issues." Through therapy it was reinforced in my mind that my wife and I had to: 1) work together, and 2) learn to communicate better. In other words, we had to both contribute to the health of the marriage. What I heard and embraced was that "marriage is the mutual contribution" of two parties: I give and she gives. My focus had been on my interpretation of how she was not giving. My focus had been on her and her faults.

After years of pain, I had to switch the lens and ask, "What did I do to contribute to this crisis?" This thoroughly ran against my previous unhealthy culture of "blame." When my focus was on how I perceived my wife's part in the marital crisis, I was stuck with an unhealthy obsession that would not allow healing. It was then that I made the decision that I was not going to blame her for our marriage crisis but would place blame on the only person I could control and change: myself.

I changed the lens from seeing an equal partnership of mutually contributing to the marriage to one where the health of it was dependent on my 100% effort. With a new perspective, it did not take me long to see my shortcomings. I then understood how my marriage had started to enter into crisis, to the point of possible divorce. God wanted to shape and change my character. It was only when I became accountable to this principle that healing would take place.

4) Seek a path of humility; repent of pride.

Naturally, taking full responsibility for a deteriorating marriage can only be achieved if one is committed to the place of self-emptying. Humility is allusive. Repentance is fleeting. Yet, these two concepts were embraced as a step in the healing path of marital health.

For leaders in the church, we can often wax eloquently about the place of humility and repentance in the life of the church—but our inner-core is filled with pride in our ability to communicate these concepts. In a faith that is grounded in humility and self-emptying (Phil. 2), the reality is that my practice was anything but the reality of humility. In essence, the very nature of most divorces by leaders in the church reflects on how their message is hypocritical: to embrace the gospel is to embrace a life of humility.

I reflected over the couples therapy that we had gone through. I then realized that most of it started from the point of hoping that my wife would understand her contribution to the marriage crisis. I was a narcissistic ball of pride, even in the midst of counseling.

Here is the thing: ministers know how to hide pride in veils of humility. Professional contrition is a learned part of most ministers. What I needed was a radical reflection of humility that only comes from an embrace of the Cross. This was missing in my life.

If my Savior could empty Himself in radical self-abasement, and this was a core to my faith, then I needed to follow Him in this path. Of course, that meant coming clean that: 1) I was not the person I wanted people to perceive, and 2) I needed to embrace repentance as a reality of life. I am a sinner, and as a sinner I have the capability to hurt and harm people. The good news is that admitting this allowed me to begin a path of repentance for how I had harmed my wife.

5) Keep visible in the church.

My church asked me, "Do you trust us?" With this, in a very real way, they told me that my marriage was broken. The first step to healing was for me to move out of the family home. With the nature of people—even in a larger church—it would become public that this couple, who say they love God, is now in the midst of a crisis, with the husband not living at home. The whispers of people now knowing details would surely be shouts of shame.

My natural instinct was one of withdrawal from visibility in the church, which in a larger church can be done without people noticing. Yet, I decided that this was the time that I needed the church more than ever. It was a time when the very core praxis of the church would be tested—by a person hurting in the midst of a crisis that was self-inflicted.

I was soon placed in the strange place of worshiping God by myself. I was placed in a position where my sins were now very public. One therapist told me that it would be better for me to attend a different church, where people would not know that my marriage was in crisis.

Here is the issue: Does the church allow sinners to be sinners, and allow the Savior to be a savior for sinners? For me, the easy path would have been one of avoidance or change. However, I wanted a path that revealed the outworking of my faith as not just a nifty theology, but practice.

What I found in the church was an awkwardness as people tried to see me as part of the community. In many of the groups that I was involved with, I did not openly voice the marriage crisis. It was not uncommon for couples to be involved in ministries without their partners. Thus, Wednesday after Wednesday, I would be an active part of the church's prayer meeting. I was involved in varying forms of smaller groups. I still had various visible skills and gifts that were being exercised. What I learned is that: 1) the church allowed me to be present, 2) they allowed me to be ministered to as I permitted, and 3) they accepted me as a sinner.

6) Find healthy activities that benefit the body and mind.
In the midst of the crisis, depression is often knocking on the door.

The pain of the crisis was excruciating. The pain of not being with my family, in the daily "ins-and-outs," tore me apart. It was at this time that I had to fight the depression that can easily eclipse mental health. It was at this time that unhealthy habits could creep in that would make the situation worse.

I was fortunate that I understood the need to have some outlets and activity to throw myself into in the midst of the crisis. Any activity that benefits the body and mind is a healthy one. I threw myself into running. In the midst of the crisis, when the pain was deep and penetrating, instead of medicating it with something unhealthy, I would lace up my running shoes and run. And run. And run. I wasn't running from my problems; running was a means to find clarity of them, a way to process them that benefitted my mind, body, and soul.

I remember in every one of my therapy sessions being asked, "Are you still running?" Soon I understood that the therapist did not have an interest in running, but wanted to know how I was doing. If I was running, then he could start at a different point of therapy. The autumn of the separation from my wife saw me run in four marathons. It was this healthy activity that gave me something to look forward to and kept me going in a positive direction.

Healing Can Happen

As I maintained a profile in the church, I perceived that many were wondering, "What caused the crisis in their marriage?" Naturally there are the "go-to" male-oriented reasons for a break in a relationship, namely, marital infidelity or one of a handful of commonly known addictions. For us, these common reasons for a crisis were not the source of the conflict; there was no infidelity or secret addiction. The issue for me happened over a period of time, intensified in the last years before the crisis.

Simply put, I was disobedient to one primary injunction for marital health: "Husbands, love your wives" (Eph. 5:25). When my attention was on how my wife was not "meeting my needs" as I walked the path of blame, I was not obeying this simple yet hard instruction. When did I stop loving my wife? I am not sure. It just happened as the months turned into years, and the crisis reached an apex.

The path to healing was a radical commitment to change from a path of self-love and understanding—this is where I had lived, in a world where my interests and needs were primary—and move towards loving my wife as a primary goal of my life. This path was somewhere down a long and winding road.

What I needed to do was to ask God to renew my love for my wife. I needed to repent that I was not following a very basic injunction. I needed to once again listen to my wife and show her that I loved her. I needed to embrace her "love reception" needs in order to heal and thrive in my marriage.

Many of these qualities and habits that I needed to embrace were foreign to me; given my own inclination, they were not "me." I had taken comfort in traditional cultural narratives that "men" were not verbal, and thus this provided an excuse for me to not "talk" with my wife. Yet, to love her meant that I needed to "open-up" a bit more and talk. To love her meant that I would allow her to have a part in my heart that I protected from outsiders and be vulnerable with her.

Even as I write, I know that "to love my wife" is a daily choice. It is a choice that comes from intentionally seeking her life and health first. This often means putting myself in places of trust and vulnerability.

After four plus months of separation, God brought my wife and me back to a place that we were keen to renew our marriage vows. A crisis had been diverted. God had given us another chance to reflect Him in our marriage. We lived the next four months still separated as issues of trust, love, and respect were re-created after years of neglect.

In many ways, they were months of a second courtship period in our relationship. There were many tears shed on my part of how I brought damage to my wife. Many habits needed to be formed and re-shaped. Then, God gave us the gift of full marriage, complete with a second—and better—honeymoon. The crisis was diverted. I am thankful to God for bringing health to my marriage.

Today is the Only Day that Counts

Relationships and marriage need daily care. Some two-plus years after the crisis, my wife and I are still happily married. We continue to enjoy the fruits of God's grace in healing our marriage and bringing us together again. We realize that we averted a crisis, and for this I continually offer prayers of thanksgiving to God for His grace.

As a husband and father, I am thankful that my children did not have to walk through the pain that often is part of marital discord and dissolution. I am thankful that God is one who accepts and provides a way of blessing for men like me who disobey His Word.

Nonetheless, in the midst of the thanksgiving and afterglow of renewal is the reality that marriage, and any relationship, is only as healthy as the commitment that is made to it. For me it is a daily reminder that I need to place my wife, as a cherished one, ahead of my needs and wants. At times this is a challenge, and a path of repentance needs to be renewed.

This is the reality, and while some may want something a bit more romantic for a marriage, I know that it would not take much to allow my marriage to again turn into a crisis. I need to daily love my wife, and seek her best in order to have God's blessings on my marriage. I need to remember the truth of my seminary professor's words and realize that unless I stay on the right path, my marriage could be in trouble again.

CREATE A CULTURE OF LEARNING
Submit to the Discipline of Learning in a Crisis
W. Rodman MacIlvaine III

Yellow signs on wooden sticks were posted in the yards that surrounded the church. "Save this historic neighborhood!" they screamed. Meanwhile, the neighbors banded together with a clever idea.

To take their revenge on church members for jamming vehicles in front of their homes, they would turn their sprinklers to face the streets. Sometimes sprinkler heads were precisely aimed at parked cars' windows, slightly cracked to keep cars tolerably cool in the sweltering Texas sun. At other times, the sprinklers were timed so that they came on just as parishioners scrambled to enter their cars.

Clearly, this Ft. Worth-area church and the surrounding neighborhood were deeply divided. Both were in crisis.

In another church, Jason Hamilton had just completed his morning jog. He loved his daily endorphin high which seemed like a mainstay in his busy schedule. But after this particular jog, something felt wrong. When he stepped up to the podium for his Sunday evening message, an awful sensation of dread hit. Waves of panic washed over him. Normally confident and outgoing, this felt foreign and sinister—like a fist in the gut.

After emergency room tests, a doctor came to his bedside to deliver the diagnosis. It wasn't a heart attack. He had experienced a panic attack, likely due to an overloaded schedule. In the days to come, his anxiety would morph into depression—and it would be nine months before it lifted.

Crises happen … all manner of crises. They're a part of life, and certainly part of life in ministry. Most local churches have expectations that they should function like a family (Eph. 2:19), and families certainly experience their share of crises.

What intellectual and spiritual framework provides the best approach for handling crises?

Popularized by Vince Lombardi, there is the approach of the famous inventor of the forward pass, Knute Rockne: "When the going gets tough; the tough gets going." That approach, of course, has some sound bite appeal, but it's perhaps more appropriate to a physical crisis than to spiritual or interpersonal ones.

Handling more complex crises requires a more nuanced approach, one that's appropriate for the realities of church leadership.

Without a conceptual framework for handling a crisis, many pastors and ministry leaders struggle over how to master their emotions. They often give in to cynicism and resign posts that could have been maintained with grace and an abundance mindset.

The core idea of this chapter is this: When senior leaders handle a crisis in a spirit of humility and learning, the crisis can become a defining event in the life of the leader and a chance for multiplied leadership power. To put it another way, humble learning in teams generates leadership wisdom and God-centered results.

Research on Crisis and Leadership

In their book *Leading for a Lifetime*, Warren Bennis and Robert Thomas advance a concept about crisis called *The Crucible Model*. A crucible is a laboratory container that can be super-heated for the purpose of creating chemical reactions. In Bennis and Thomas' work, the crucible metaphor describes a messy leadership environment that forges a new leadership skill.

As Bennis and Thomas performed qualitative case studies on successful leaders, they noticed an unexpected trend. The most successful leaders encountered a significant crisis or series of crises that became foundational to the rest of their career. Moreover, they found that the crisis could be transformative, regardless of age or cultural background.

As Bennis and Thomas reviewed the various crises in their subject group, they discovered that for a crisis to be transformative it had to: 1) bring more pain than they thought they could endure, 2) force them to address issues in their lives that limited their current leadership, and 3) create a new and fresh leadership story.

Bennis and Thomas were so confident about their *crucible theory* of leadership that they rather boldly asserted, "We have developed a theory that describes, we believe for the first time, how leaders come to be" (p. 4).

By dubbing their model, *the crucible model*, they reinforce the notion that crisis often brings chaos. In the crucible there is tumult of unpredictability and pain. Often there are no discernible solutions at the time, and hope for a better future seems lost. But the notion of the crucible suggests that the leader is being shaped and formed in fresh ways toward an unexpected future.

Bennis and Thomas suggest that the outcome of the crucible is not only new learning but a fresh story, and "story" is very important to their theory. After the crucible, the leaders are more reflective about their crisis. They can describe what things were like *before* the crisis, how they were shaped *in* the crisis, and what life is like *now,* as a result of the crisis.

The leader's story then becomes an inspirational tale, reminding followers that crises shape authenticity and trustworthiness in the leader. One of the great benefits of coming through a crisis is fresh authenticity that comes with being at the end of your rope. They then find new hope which helps to forge a new future.

Biblical Examples of the Crucible Theory

What Bennis and Thomas have discovered through case study research is also clearly seen in the great leaders of the Bible.

- Abraham is the father of faith, one of our greatest examples of trust (Rom. 4:18-19). But God produces exemplar faith in Abraham by allowing him to go into the crucible of waiting on God. He waits decades to receive the promise of a son. And he dies still waiting on promises that will come to his descendents (Heb. 11:39-40).

- Moses becomes a man of great humility by shouldering a titanic leadership load that was arguably as great, *or greater*, than any other in the ancient world (Num. 12:3).

- David becomes a man after God's own heart, in part because of the near decade-long persecution he endured at the hands of his father-in-law, King Saul (1 Sam. 18:10ff).

- Elijah becomes a powerful prophet even through his anxiety and depression (1 Kings 17-19). The results of Elijah's learning *in crucible* become inspirational to Elisha who seemed to receive a double portion of Elijah's power (2 Kings 2:9).

- Daniel becomes a powerful leader in secular Babylon, in part through the crucible of having been ripped from his family at a young age and then exercising radical faith in God (Dan. 1-4).

- Nehemiah is shaped as a leader through the constant opposition that came as he was rebuilding the walls of Jerusalem (Neh. 1-4).

- Paul became stronger through his thorn in the flesh (2 Cor. 12:7-10).

- Jesus has the greatest crucible story of all. Because He was obedient to the place of death, God highly exalted Him and gave Him the greatest name (Phil. 2:5-11).

Each of these biblical characters was shaped through one or more crucibles. Not only were they broken by the crucible, but they did something quite strategic in the crucible. They engaged in a humble God-ward learning experience in which they were able to fellowship with God and learn new things about how to lead in the process.

Historical Examples of the Crucible Theory

Some of the greatest leaders in the history of the church have encountered the same refining process in the crucible of crisis. In each case, an unexpected crucible became an occasion for God-ward learning, and, in the process, God sovereignly guided them into places of greater ministry effectiveness.

Martin Luther suffered in multiple ways during the protestant reformation. Physically, he struggled with recurring kidney stones, migraine headaches, digestive problems and ear infections (just to name a few of his medical maladies).

Emotionally, he faced the rejection of peers, who were sometimes supportive of him in private, but turned against him in public. And of course, he faced the revulsion of the religious authorities who, with vicious anger, sought to kill him. Spiritually, Luther often felt the weight of spiritual warfare.

Nevertheless, Luther, embracing Psalm 119:17 as his inspiration, determined he would learn theology and leadership *experientially* through his suffering. For Luther, suffering and crisis were occasions to learn from the sovereign God.

The remarkable story of Elizabeth Elliott suggests the same commitment to learn in the midst of crisis. In 1956, Jim Elliott and his four colleagues were preparing to meet with the Auca Indians, with the intent to build a ministry among them. Shortly after their plane landed, they were ambushed. All five were quickly killed and a young Elizabeth Elliott was bereft of her husband.

It would be humanly understandable if she grew bitter and distant from God after such a devastating tragedy. But in the crucible of her grief, she became a learner. Within the year, she determined to return and continue to work among the tribe that took the life of her husband. In time, her husband's killer came to Christ and became a leader in the fledgling church. Her story has inspired many leaders, but at its core it's a story of leadership born out of a crucible—and in the crucible she committed to learn from God.

Barriers to Learning in Crisis

We should note, however, that many Christian leaders do not submit to the discipline of learning in the context of a crisis.

There are two common reasons for this. First, many pastors and senior ministry leaders fear they will be judged by their congregations. Indeed, many North American congregations have a culture of inauthenticity that causes them to demand near problem-free living from their leaders.

Pastors are expected to never be discouraged or depressed. Physical problems are okay, but emotional problems seem anathema. If a leader is discouraged, it is assumed that he has a spiritual problem. If a leader confesses to bouts with lust, greed, anger and all the other normal temptations in life, the church may conclude that this leader is not the right leader.

Second, there is an implied prosperity theology in many churches that suggests that if you're doing all you should be doing in ministry, you will prosper in ways that the particular culture expects: Church growth will always maintain the right trajectory. Leaders will be shielded from certain problems and there will be a certain degree of success.

If congregational leaders are not willing to accept that God shapes and molds His leaders through crucibles, then they will not get the learning from their pastors that creates the authenticity that accelerates spiritual growth.

Recent Research About Types of Crises

In my research, I have identified eight common crucibles that church leaders typically encounter during the course of their ministries. These eight crucibles are not meant to be an exhaustive list, but they are the common ones that show up in interviews and counseling.

The first crucible church leaders often face is a *spiritual crisis*. The leader comes to a place of doubt about some aspect of theology or even the goodness of God. During the crisis phase, he encounters a personal "dark night of the soul." As he begins to resolve this issue, he thinks differently about the mission of the church. His desire is now to serve as Jesus served and lead others in the process.

A *cultural crisis* is a second personal crucible ministry leaders may confront. A leader may experience frustration that the North American church, in general—and his church, in particular—are failing to engage the postmodern culture with relevant expressions of ministry. As the leader and his team wrestle with this for their own church, they become open to God leading them into a new kind of ministry that meets tangible needs of people fed up with church. There is a growing cluster of authors such as Dan Kimball, David Kinnaman, Gabe Lyons, and David Olson who are deeply concerned that the church has failed to engage the postmodern culture.

Church consultant Milfred Minatrea highlighted the leader crucible of *mid-life crisis* during a 2007 interview. This third crucible also called "the half-time crisis" is when the leader thinks, "I've given the bulk of my ministry years to a consumeristic flock who constantly demands more. What am I going to do in my remaining years to advance the kingdom?"

An *interpersonal crisis* is a fourth crucible. A senior leader will clash with a ministry partner. This conflict crushes expectations and creates tremendous pain. As the leader works through that pain, he comes to see his ministry in a different light. This seems to have been the experience of Dieter Zander at Willow Creek Community Church according to Gibbs and Bolger in their book *Emerging Churches* (pp. 323-328).

A fifth common crucible is the *moral crisis or potential moral crisis*. A senior leader confronts the presence of a habit in his life that is out of control. As he effectively engages this struggle, he begins to minister from the vantage point of the healing he has experienced. For instance, Chuck Colson, a convicted yet released felon, began Prison Fellowship as a way to serve prisoners and transform the prison system. Further, many pastors who have started Celebrate Recovery ministries in their churches have done so because they detected the presence of an addictive habit in their lives. They now minister out of the strength of their recovery. Their authenticity causes a culture of genuine maturity to flourish in their congregations.

A *situational crisis*, the sixth crucible, is when a church that once occupied a vibrant place in an urban area is now surrounded by poverty and pain. Or a church that was once focused, stalls out. The pastor thinks, "Do we move the church? Do we shift our vision? Or, do we stay and minister—*missionally*—in the place where God has placed us?"

For example, College Hill Presbyterian Church, located in Cincinnati, Ohio, moved toward missional ministry during a crisis brought on by denominational conflict. In his book, *Can the Church Be Converted: How "Missional" Came to College Hill Presbyterian Church*, Stephen Eyre suggests that when casting vision during the crisis, "The missional process is the shift from the church as an institution in a Christian culture, to a community in mission in a non-Christian culture" (pp. 6-10). Lois Barrett, in her book, *Treasure in Clay Jars: Patterns in Missional Faithfulness*, also suggests that crisis is a common precipitating cause for missional change. "A congregation's sense that it has a missional vocation, and its idea of what that vocation is, comes about out of the crucible of struggle" (p. 53).

A *health crisis* occurs when the leader, or a member of a leader's family, goes through a predicament of physical or mental distress that requires extensive treatment. As Lon Solomon suggests in his book, *Brokenness: How God Redeems Pain and Suffering*, this seventh crucible causes the leader to be much more sensitive to others with similar health issues.

The eighth crucible church leaders may face is a *managed crisis*. For example, Chase Oaks Church in Plano, Texas moved toward a new form of ministry through a managed crisis. At the beginning of their transition, they faced five challenges: an imminent pastoral change, a location change, a name change, a shift in worship and a realignment of ministries. The convergence of these issues certainly constituted a crisis. Through skillful management of these challenges, they were able to move in a fresh direction.

Of the eight, the one I hear popping up more and more is *the dark night of the soul* as highlighted in the *spiritual crucible*. To be a pastor and go through a *dark night of the soul* means that you are in a lonely place. But many pastors suggest that it was in this very place that they sensed God in new and powerful ways. In time, they were able to articulate this—and it was a source of fresh leadership in their ministries.

A Personal Example

We faced a serious crisis in our church between 2003 and 2006 that was transformative in my leadership.

My wife and I were part of the team that founded Grace Community Church in Bartlesville, Oklahoma in 1995. At the time, Cindy and I were in our thirties with four young kids and two dogs. Our core group consisted of six couples. All of us were at the same phase of life, with young kids, and each of us had been immersed in campus ministries in college. We knew what it was like to be discipled and then go disciple someone else. It was a very strong team.

For the first seven years, we enjoyed strong and consistent growth.

Our opening service took place in September, 1995, and we spent two years as guests at a local community college. But after two years, our church was straining the resources of the college.

One night, during a marathon elder meeting, we sensed God calling us to build a building … a daunting task to be sure! We were just 75 families at that point. But we had a strong sense of direction, so we took the plunge and made plans. On the Sunday that the pledges came in, we were amazed. The pledges were far beyond what we expected, with a guaranteed loan of twice that amount.

This didn't seem possible, and we felt the pleasure of God upon us. We completed the building two years later and moved in on Easter Sunday, 1999. To our amazement, about 600 people packed into our auditorium, and nearly 400 spilled into our atrium and kids' area. As you can imagine, we were hugely fired up by the response of the community, and again, we felt the pleasure of God upon us.

Then things changed!

In late 2002, the Phillips Petroleum Company merged with Conoco Oil. That meant that the headquarters for the new company would be in Houston, Texas. People in our city were in shock. Bartlesville had been a one-corporate town for over 100 years. Bartlesville had been identified with Phillips for as long as anyone could remember.

Within the year, we figure we lost 40% of our congregation. These were our key leaders … some were elders. They were the carriers of our vision. It was devastating.

Moreover, for the next three and a half years, our city struggled to forge a new identity. The population of our city didn't change appreciably, nor did the numbers in our church change appreciably. But there was a vision drain in the city and in our church.

We descended into a three-year, painful crucible.

In the meantime, God did something that was completely unanticipated.

He opened doors for us to plant churches internationally.

In the late 1990s, we assisted in planting two churches in central Russia. Five years later, in early 2003, our construction teams had completed the work. We felt we should go somewhere else. We determined to work in Cuba.

I flew to Cuba with a friend, not knowing a soul on the island. All I knew is that we wanted to make contact with church planters and partner with them. In one of the most nondescript areas of the island, I met two people: Pastor Elisio and Pastor Roberto.

These men had been actively praying about launching a church planting movement. They had no resources—and it would take a Class-A miracle—but they were praying. In fact, they'd already trained church planters, in faith that it would happen. We met them through some extremely unlikely circumstances. They considered us to be the supernatural answer to their prayers.

From 2003 to 2008, we had the privilege of planting over fifty churches in central Cuba. After that, we started a church planter training school. If anyone had tried to tell me that we'd be instrumental in planting fifty churches in five years, I would have laughed and said, "Right! How?" Our Cuban partners shouldered the load. They worked harder and smarter than we could ever have imagined. As they ran the race, we were their coaches and mentors.

We structured our school so that highly motivated church planters could get equipped in twelve months. When they graduated, they started a church under the spiritual and logistical leadership of the director of the school.

Our most successful graduate had been in jail from the age of 16 to 26. That meant he had no opportunity for traditional education! But he's an amazing leader, and our model of education was just what he needed.

So think about this: While our city was struggling with vision, and while our church was struggling with vision, relative to our city, the Lord opened up tremendous doors internationally. By God's grace, we were presiding over a church planting movement in Central Cuba.

In our crucible we noticed something.

The churches being planted under our leadership were all missional, but not because we planned it that way. We weren't even using the term missional at the time. They were missional because to reach people in Cuba, you have to meet tangible needs with a show of overwhelming love.

So we started learning from our Cuban partners. Then we started asking, "What would happen if we did ministry in our city just like we do ministry in Cuba?"

Then we gained some traction with this. In mid-2005, the elders encouraged me to go on a study-sabbatical. I'd been at Grace for ten years, and they said, "You can go anywhere you want … one month."

I chose the University of Oxford. I spent one week at Keble Hall, taking classes with the organization led by Ravi Zacharias, and a second week at Wycliffe Hall, taking courses from Alister McGrath and his team.

The first day of classes, I paused to pray in the beautiful chapel at Keble Hall and was flooded with an impression from God (not audible but strong, nonetheless): "I want you to go back to school, and I want you to get a doctorate."

When I arrived at Dallas Theological Seminary in the summer of 2006, I was part of the large church cohort. On day one, I again sensed a strong impression from God: "Do your dissertation on how to transition existing churches in a missional direction." This is what we were experiencing in Cuba. This is what I sensed we needed for our city.

God graciously used my D.Min. studies to equip me to lead a missional movement at Grace Community Church. We needed enough speed to capture opportunities, but also needed enough patience to bring people along.

By late 2006, our city had coalesced around a new identity. It was becoming more diverse and was growing with a lot of younger IT professionals.

At the same time, we formed a team for the re-visioning process. Our team met for two hours on Saturdays. We prayed and hammered out a new vision—with missional language and missional intent.

When we pitched the vision to the congregation, it seemed like a natural extension of how God was already leading us. From 2007 to present, we went full bore into a total missional reorientation.

Four Examples

First, we sought targeted opportunities to serve institutions in our city. And we did this in the spirit of Jeremiah 29:7, *"Seek the welfare of the city for in it you will have welfare."* So we sought the welfare of the city. We renovated teachers' lounges in the public schools. We delivered meals to city workers.

We helped teachers move into their classrooms as school was starting. We cleaned up after local flooding devastated neighborhoods. We did tutoring in the schools. We did mentoring in the jails ... especially with female prisoners who wanted to be better mothers.

Members of our church organized to start a hospice house for people facing end-of-life issues. We ministered to abused girls who were also cognitively impaired. Incredibly, every girl in that institution came to Christ. We then trained those girls to minister in retirement homes to elderly people, some of whom were also cognitively impaired.

One week we saw the stunning results of this ministry. Our cognitively impaired girls were sharing Christ with cognitively impaired senior adults, leading them to Christ and encouraging them in the faith.

A second category of missional work involved the arts. We championed the arts because God is the consummate artist—and many artists have been hurt by organized religion.

Northeastern Oklahoma has historically been a significant arts community, so we sponsored an annual event called *Artfest*. We had a biblical theme and the artists had to explain how their works fit into that biblical theme. We gave cash awards at a reception that became a community event. Sometimes our state congressman showed up and we had well-known artists from other states attend.

Every year, I've had the opportunity to share the gospel with guests, simply by explaining the meaning of one of our paintings. This art brought us tremendous good will in the community. People seemed to assume that if we were a church that loved the arts, then we must have been a church that sought the betterment of the city.

A third example is that we had a reputation for serving other churches and other pastors—with no strings attached. In Cuba, we learned that we were good at ministering to and uniting pastors. The leader in our church who excelled at this was our former executive pastor, Ed Schmidt. Ed served as XP during our missional transition and has been my ministry partner in Cuba for over a decade.

In Cuba, we started realizing the truth of D.L. Moody's famous statement, "It's amazing what God can do through you when you don't care who gets the credit." So we started proactively helping other churches in our city. In one case, we provided a church with our worship leader to launch a new worship service. In another case, we helped a church reformulate an elder board.

Why could we look outward to do this? By God's grace, we paid off our building. With no debt, we determined that we would provide servant leadership in the city by helping smaller churches with bi-vocational pastors. If we did it in Cuba, why couldn't we do it here?

A fourth example is our Celebrate Recovery ministry. This has transformed the culture of our church in the direction of much greater authenticity. My wife started CR seven years ago. She is now a state representative and oversees about a dozen CR chapters in the northeastern Oklahoma area.

When we started CR, Cindy and I determined we would work the steps together. Just working the steps has revolutionized our marriage. Now we share our story openly. The culture of authenticity at Grace has made our church more like a hospital for the hurting than a hotel for the self-satisfied. This sense of authenticity has greatly enhanced our missional vision.

Wisdom Gained in the Midst of Our Crisis

The years of 2003-2006 were our crucible years but were also an occasion for learning. While we didn't do it perfectly, we sought to approach our crucible in a spirit of humility and discovery in dependence on the Spirit's guidance.

Today I place the leadership insights from our crucible into three categories.

First, we learned to view ministry in North America from the vantage point of the developing world.

If you read current North American demographers, sociologists and church growth pundits, you can get discouraged. They're all saying that the North American church is declining.

On the other hand, the church is exploding in the developing world. Lamin Sanneh of Yale University is a former Muslim—now a convert to Catholicism. In his book, *Disciples of All Nations*, he says we're currently in the midst of a third great awakening (pp. 272-73).

Andrew Walls in his work, *The Missionary Movement in Christian History* speaks glowingly of the expansion of the faith in Africa (p. 79ff)... so too Thomas Oden, in *How Africa Shaped the Christian Mind* (p. 112ff), Rodney Stark, in the *Triumph of Christianity* (pp. 353-387) and Philip Jenkins, *The Next Christendom* in chapters 1 and 10.

Mark Hutchinson's *Short History of Global Evangelicalism* seeks to make sense of what the numbers really are. He asks, "Are these huge numbers really accurate?" He shows how we get the large numbers, and he affirms that, yes, there is a Christ-movement that is sweeping the planet (pp. 209-238, 259ff).

But how is the Christian faith exploding? It would appear it's exploding through service.

Donald E. Miller of USC received a grant to do a multi-country study of global Pentecostalism. He's a self-described liberal-Episcopalian. At the beginning, he thought he'd find craziness in the Pentecostal-Evangelical movement. But he didn't. What he found was totally counterintuitive. He and co-author Tetsunao Yamamori in their writing, *Global Pentecostalism: The New Face of Christian Social Engagement*, found that the common element in global Pentecostalism was compassionate social engagement (pp. 99ff). They found missional churches that were leading people to Jesus in the context of service.

In his Princeton lecture, he said that if you want to know who is really engaging in compassionate service around the world, it's the Pentecostal-Evangelicals; they share Christ in the context of missional ministry.

In our crucible at Grace Community Church, we discovered that if we want to grow a strong church in North America, we have to approach that city as if we were going to a city in Africa, China, or India. We have to learn the indigenous culture of our own city, and then we have to mobilize servers.

Second, we learned that high participation worship facilitates love for God, as well as the missional ministry we sought.
When we made our missional transition, we also changed the way we did worship. We set candles on either side of our auditorium, and I said this: "If God has answered a prayer for you in the past week, we invite you to come forward and light a candle to celebrate answered prayer and put it on the stage."

At first, I thought maybe five people would do this. Not so! We had a line of people wanting to come forward and light candles. People love to do something with their bodies in worship: stand, raise hands, or move their bodies. There's nothing magical about lighting a candle. It doesn't make God more likely to answer prayer. But so much of worship in the Old Testament involved the use of the whole body. Lighting candles fit into that sense of purpose.

At this point, we sometimes have whole families come forward to light candles. They put them on the stage and then can go to a place in the auditorium where they can kneel and pray. There are some weeks when our auditorium is full of activity during worship. Sometimes people come to prayer stations with friends to pray about a burden.

At the same time, we started putting communion elements on benches in the front. People could come up and serve themselves communion—the communion benches were low, so they had to kneel. Maybe a handful of people wanted to get served the old fashioned way, but most people loved the sense of putting their body into worship.

We discovered that people who had been un-churched loved this. They felt there was a sense of spirituality about the services that got them in touch with something beyond themselves.

A third lesson we learned: When you think about planting and building a church, it's important to think influence, not numbers.

It's easy for pastors to see competing churches post big numbers and think, "Man, I've got to post bigger." That's the wrong idea!

The right idea is to think "influence," and then ask the question, "How can I influence our city in a Godward direction, according to what He's really doing ... right now? How can I equip people in my church for more impactful ministry?"

When I was working on my dissertation and looking at potential churches for case studies, I heard stories that pained me. Pastors were emphatic that they weren't numbers driven or money driven. But values expressed in conversations indicated the opposite. Their tweets assumed a consumer approach to ministry.

When you think about influence, it opens up radically different ideas about ministry strategy and ministry measurements. For us it came back to evangelism—in the context of serving relationships in the city—and it came back to discipleship. Evangelism and discipleship almost sound old-school. But when we assessed where our overseas ministry partners were excelling, it went back to that: evangelism and discipleship. But there was always this caveat: the evangelism and discipleship had to be highly tailored to the culture in which the church was growing.

Conclusion

Crises happen. They're a part of life. They're a part of ministry. It's not a matter of *if* they will come, but *when*. The best leaders are those that have a framework for handling crises—that framework should include a capacity for humble learning in the midst of the crisis. When humble learning takes place, God seems to energize that pastor or senior leader toward a new place of authenticity and leadership power.

LEADING CHANGE IN A CULTURE RESISTANT TO CHANGE

Lessons from the Philippines Speak to Us All

Stephen G. Tan

Although the first parts of this chapter might lead you to think that the content is just for international or Chinese churches, there are valuable lessons for all churches, everywhere, to be gleaned from Stephen's words. ~ Editor

Chinese Churches in the Philippines

In Metro Manila, many of the younger generation are leaving the Chinese churches in droves, either disillusioned with church or heading to ethnic Filipino churches.

This trend is so alarming that many in the Chinese Christian community are asking if there is still a need for ethnic Chinese churches in the Philippines. The answer is *"Yes!"* with more than a million ethnic Chinese in the Philippines still needing to hear the gospel, many of whom are fiercely Chinese in their culture.

So why are so many Chinese churches not more effective in reaching out to the next generation of unbelieving Chinese? Why are they having such a difficult time convincing their own second or third generation Christian children to remain at their home church and serve? In my estimation, the Chinese church will disappear from the Philippines in 40-50 years without the next generation's interest to carry it on. There is an urgency to address this issue *now!*

Without getting into the intricacies of cultural and generational nuances involved in this question, one major factor that prevents Chinese-Filipino churches from adapting quickly to the changing needs of the new generation is the fact that the Chinese culture is a culture traditionally adverse to change.

Aversion to Change

Being ethnically Chinese—born in the Philippines, but raised in Texas—I remember asking my parents why we had to follow certain Chinese traditions that made no sense to me. Their answer was, "This is what the Chinese have been doing for 5,000 years … and who can argue with 5,000 years of history." This answer encapsulates the general sentiments of our culture—a culture adverse to change.

To be fair, there are certain Chinese cultural influences that are worth keeping and should not change, such as respect for the elders, love for the family, and a strong sense of community and tradition. But change is inevitable.

Many Chinese-Filipino churches were started by Chinese Christian converts—first-generation immigrants born in mainland China or born to parents who emigrated from China. Almost everyone spoke Hookien Chinese in the home and church. But as the second- and third-generation youth grew up, they partially assimilated with the mostly western Filipino culture, having studied in predominately Filipino universities and worked with Filipinos in multi-national corporations.

While culturally Chinese, the next generation preferred a western style of worship, as well as a more "professional" and technology-embracing means of organizing the church. Hence, a cultural and generational clash ensued. Since the church board was usually dominated by the older elders and deacons, the changes proposed by the next generation were not taken into consideration.

For example, many Chinese churches were afraid that using English in the worship service would take away from the "Chineseness" of the church. Only when many young people began leaving did these churches decide to translate services. Many in the older generation feared the loss of their language would result in a loss of cultural identity. This was also the situation in immigrant Chinese churches in the U.S. and Canada which led to great generational and cultural conflicts.

The Chinese churches in the Philippines reluctantly allowed English-only worship services when the younger generation, tired of listening to translated services, began the next wave of departure.

The aversion to any significant change in adapting to the cultural needs of the next generation led many to leave the Chinese churches which they grew up in. Then, because of a lack of young people, there was an inability to attract the unchurched next generation.

Grace Christian Church of the Philippines (GCCP) was in a similar situation as the other Chinese churches in the Philippines. With over forty years of history, the church was not changing fast enough to position itself to reach out to the unchurched, to disciple its own members, and to meet the spiritual needs of the next generation. However, since 2002, by the grace of God, it has grown from being a mid-sized Chinese church to perhaps the largest Chinese church in the Philippines.

What happened?

Apart from the work of the Holy Spirit, leading culture change in a church culture that doesn't like change was the key to our growth as a church.

Grace Christian Church of the Philippines

The entire Grace Christian Ministries—which includes Grace Bible Church (1949), Grace Christian High School (1950), Grace Gospel Church (1952), and Grace Christian Church (1968)—was started in 1949 by Mrs. Julia L. Tan, a widow with five small children. A devout Christian and a trained educator, God had placed a vision in the heart of Mrs. Tan to bring the gospel to the Chinese in the Philippines through Christian education. Unlike North America, where the majority of families who send their children to Christian schools come from Christian families, in the Philippines, 70% to 80% of families who send their children to Christian schools are from unbelieving families. Therefore, the Christian school in the Philippines is primarily an evangelistic vehicle.

Mrs. Julia Tan started Grace Christian High School in 1950 and the school quickly outgrew its first location. The school moved from its location in Manila to a new location in Quezon City, a suburb of Manila in 1966.

That weekend, Grace Christian Church started Sunday church worship services in two classrooms of the school to minister to the new community. It is unique in the traditional sense that the school, in effect, started the church. However, there is a biblical example in Acts 19:9 when Paul started a church by ministering in the school of Tyrannus.

This model of a church and school was rooted in Mrs. Tan's training under foreign missionaries in her hometown of Xiamen, China. That model led her to adopt two slogans for Grace Christian High School and Church: (a) The school is the church's mission field, and the church is the school's spiritual home, and (b) Separate administration—united harvest field.

In early 1967, Mrs. Julia Tan asked her son (and my father), Rev. Paul Lee Tan, to return after his theological studies, at Dallas Theological Seminary and Grace Theological Seminary in the United States, to help pastor and develop the church. In June 1967, he returned to the Philippines to be the church's first pastor. In less than two years, the congregation grew organically, from less than 30 people to over 100 members, comprised of Grace Christian High School teachers, students and parents. A church constitution was drafted and the time came to formally inaugurate the little church.

In October 1968, Grace Christian Church was formally inaugurated with Rev. Paul Lee Tan being ordained and installed as the first senior pastor.

Issues of Leadership

When our family migrated to the U.S. in 1983, five different pastors led the church over the next twenty years. With the length of pastorates ranging from one to eight years, the church could not sustain any momentum for the changes needed to take the church into the twenty-first century.

At its height during this period, the church had 500 to 600 adults and children in weekly attendance. While this was considered a good-sized church by the standards of the Chinese-Filipino churches, the basic need for developing a culture of change, to enhance growth and effectiveness, was not achieved.

From 2003 to 2005, the church was without a senior pastor and church attendance dropped. At the request of my father, from 2002 to 2005 I served as a visiting pastor, helping primarily with pulpit supply and analyzing the needs of the church. It was apparent from my background as a management consultant that what the church needed was culture change. In 2005, I was called by the church to serve as the lead pastor.

Unique Factors that Allowed for Change

There were two unique factors that allowed me to implement the changes. The first factor was desperation. The church was so desperate to find a lead pastor that they were willing to invite a 28-year-old to serve in the position. Ironically, I was eligible to serve as their senior pastor but would not have qualified to serve as a deacon (minimum age of 30).

The desperation for change was evident in this conversation I had with an older lady in the church during one of my first weeks in the new pastorate. She asked me, "Pastor, will you be like the other pastors who promise to stay forever but end up staying 2-3 years, abandoning us to go to the U.S.?" The previous five lead pastors had all immigrated to the U.S. I told her in my broken Hookien Chinese, "Auntie, don't you worry about that, I came *from* the U.S. and have no plans on going back anytime soon."

I have to admit the temptation was strong to have a "fall back" plan with a church or ministry opportunity in the U.S. If this pastorate didn't work out, I could always return back home. I thought as a missionary, I could justify having regular furloughs to go back to the U.S. and, during that time could look for another job if I wanted to. However, I knew that if I were to embark on lasting culture change in this church, I had an obligation to see it through. So, in order to avoid the temptation of returning back to the U.S. if this "experiment" failed, my wife and I made the decision to not raise monetary support from the U.S. as a typical missionary. Instead, we decided to go to the Philippines, take a local pastor's salary and live as everyone else. For us, this was a leap of faith.

The church had gone through so much difficulty and hardships that the desperate atmosphere was primed for a change. In other words, they were willing to try anything to become a relevant church again. They just needed someone bold enough to lead them. And if it failed, the last pastor would be the one to blame.

It was not an ideal situation. When I arrived, the church didn't even have enough money to pay their electricity bill. When there is no money what can you do? The only thing to do is trust God.

The second factor that allowed me to lead a culture change was the church's major shift in governance structure. This organizational realignment allowed the church with a storied history to implement the changes needed for reaching the next generation.

Grace Christian Church's original constitution and bylaws were drafted in 1968 with a congregational approach to church governance influenced by the school's baptistic background. School co-founder Dr. Edwin Spahr was a member of the Association of Baptists for World Evangelism. Thus, GCCP was primarily congregational in governance with provisions for a board of elders and a board of deacons.

However, in the early eighties, challenges escalated between the pastors and the lay-board. In March 1983, a revision to the church constitution and bylaws was passed by the congregation, shifting the church governance from a congregational to a pastor/elder-led structure. More specifically, the constitutional change stipulated that the senior pastor was to chair the church board. This gave the senior pastor the legal means to set the church's agenda and effectively lead the church, while still maintaining accountability to the board.

This idea of a pastor-led church, but accountable to the board, finds biblical support. Dr. Gene Getz in *Elders and Leaders* points out, "The New Testament definitely teaches and illustrates that when there is a plurality of leadership, someone needs to function as the primary leader of the team" (p. 217). Additionally, Gerald Cowen in *Who Rules the Church? Examining Congregational Leadership and Church Government* argues that this primary leader should be the pastor. The pastor has the God-given authority to lead the church.

If a lay leader is made the primary leader of the board, then it could cause some problems. Anthony notes in *The Effective Church*

Board, "The chairperson of the board controls the church and the members of the church staff, in spite of the possibility that this leader may possess little (if any) spiritual training" (p. 108).

Also, if a lay leader has power over the pastor then the pastor may be unwilling to admonish or rebuke that individual or another elder at the risk of losing his job. Anthony further states, "The deacons [lay individuals] mentioned in the Book of Acts were not elected to tell the apostles how to conduct their ministries" (p. 107). A team leadership model, with a pastor as the primary leader, is an efficient and scripturally-supported model for effective leading and governance.

Gene Getz illustrates this model of church leadership in his Fellowship Bible Churches. Dr. Getz served as the primary leader and chairman of the board of elders while also being accountable to other elders (p. 255).

After another minor change in the constitution in 2008, Grace Christian Church had officially moved from a congregational-led church to an elder-led church. The six members of the board of elders would lead the overall thrust of the church, especially with regard to the spiritual direction. The twenty-eight members of the board of deacons would govern the administrative policies of the church. Within the board of elders, the senior pastor would serve as the leader and first among equals of this group, yet accountable to the board of elders.

Although the journey from a congregation-led model to an elder-led model for church governance at Grace Christian Church certainly did not happen overnight, its change was essential to allow for the growth these past four years. With godly, spiritual men—who loved Christ and His church—serving alongside the pastor, the church was able to make the changes necessary to continue to be a lighthouse to the Chinese community of Metro Manila in the twenty-first century.

Let's now look at the changes that began to shift the culture of the church.

Change #1: Numbers, Numbers, Numbers
While this may be a great generalization, Asians love numbers and the Chinese really love numbers. Numbers are the measure of your

success. Here in Asia, there is a competition to have the most material things, the most money, the most children, etc. This love for numbers and its definition for success made its way into the Chinese churches in the Philippines. The number of people in your congregation determined your relevance and your effectiveness. It also determined your own congregation's perspective, as well as that of those on the outside. In our church's weekly bulletin we had all our attendance numbers written out—not only for the worship service, but also for each weekly event.

A church that is trying to make a culture change must start with small changes. To wean ourselves off of using numbers as a metric to determine our "success," I asked that the attendance of each church event be taken off the weekly bulletin. We would not get caught up playing the numbers game. In hindsight it served another purpose: the bulletin would not show the dip in attendance when these changes were made. If it were there, someone who wasn't ready for a change could have easily pointed out the drop in attendance and say things were not working.

Along with removing the attendance numbers from the bulletin, we also removed all the things which were not relevant to the edification of those coming. We removed the amount of the weekly offering from the bulletin. We would trust the Lord by faith for His financial provisions. Those who wanted to know what the weekly offering was could come into the church accounting office and find out. There was still transparency. We even removed who would be the next week's speaker so that they would not decide on attending the following week based on the speaker they wanted to hear.

You might think the removal of numbers would not be an issue, but there was an outcry. Nonetheless, I stood firm in our decision not to publicize our attendances and other numerical metrics in the church bulletin. Nowadays, outside of the board—which does track numerical metrics for a wide variety of items—the congregation doesn't look for a number to measure our success as a church.

Change #2: Getting Back to the Basics
Prior to my coming, the church seemed to try desperately to grow and become relevant by trying all sorts of new methods.

Whatever was viewed as the latest ministry "fad," such as

the Purpose Driven Life or Willow Creek's seeker-sensitive model, would often be adopted "lock, stock and barrel," without theological and contextual factors being taken into consideration. In the process of introducing these "models" for explosive church growth, the Chinese churches were losing their identity and, most importantly, what it meant to be the church. Furthermore, those who were more traditional and culturally sensitive thought that any changes would mean adopting a more western approach to ministry and, as a result, resisted change.

That is why when I came, I told the staff and board that our change would come by getting back to the basics. We would not employ any known church growth model. Instead, we would see if there was anything in those models that we could adapt for our cultural context. Most importantly, we would go back to the basics of seeing what Scripture has to say about what a church is to be.

We narrowed the purpose of our church to the key elements of what a church is to do—*Evangelize—Disciple—Repeat*. Nothing fancy, nothing gimmicky, nothing to attract but simply to get back to the basics of what Scripture reminds us.

This was important in a culture that didn't want to change. If we had employed a church growth model fashioned after U.S. churches, those who didn't want to change would charge that we were becoming too "westernized." But since the principles in Scripture preceded even that of our own Chinese culture, we could tell them that we must follow Christ first, before following our Chinese culture.

If there was something that didn't scripturally jive with our culture, then it was God's Word that won out. By focusing on strong, biblically-based preaching, teaching, caring, and children's ministry, the church was on its way towards a revival. The people started coming, challenged and convicted by the living Word of God.

Returning to the basics also included embracing the original heritage and vision of the church. The vision of the church was to primarily reach out to the Chinese in the Philippines. But the simple fact is that the Chinese are a hard ethnic group to reach. Many of them have deep-seated cultural and familial animosities and wrong assumptions about Christianity. Many thought that turning to Christ would be a total abandonment of their cultural identity. Others were simply "too successful" to contemplate a spiritual need in their lives or were hesitant to risk angering the gods who may, in turn, bring them bad luck.

There were many who thought that we should no longer focus on reaching out primarily to the Chinese, reaching out to the ethnic Filipinos instead. They are certainly more receptive to the gospel. However, with so few Chinese churches already—and many of them dying—if we ceased to intentionally reach out to the Chinese, who would reach the immigrants who continue to come? Who would reach out to the older generations who considered themselves Chinese? Who would minister to the new generation that straddles both cultures? We needed to return to our historical roots and challenge the congregation about our special and unique calling.

Another reason why the church was started was to specifically minister to the unchurched families of our sister school, Grace Christian High School. Unlike Christian schools in the United States, 70 to 80% of the families who sent their children to the school were non-Christian. They were Buddhist, Taoist, Atheists, Agnostics— or a mixture of everything, which is quite common in pantheistic southeast Asia.

However, because of some historical tensions between church and school, many in the church didn't want to focus on the open mission field that was literally right across the street. These thousands of students and their families were essentially a "captured audience" for the gospel. Perhaps God wasn't blessing our church because, while we were sorry about not evangelizing our "ends of the earth," we forgot to evangelize and reach out to our own "Jerusalem." We again embraced the heritage of our founding, reaffirmed our calling to reach out to the unchurched families and became more intentional in reaching out to them.

The Lord blessed as we saw many come to Christ and become part of our church. We accomplished this by simply going back to our most natural ministry calling and to a people group whose culture, thinking, and language we naturally understood.

Change #3: Perception Change from the Inside Out
It was very apparent when I first arrived at the church that there was a negative perception of our church, not only from the outside community, but also from within. I posed the following question to a

few church members, "Would you invite your friends to this church?" Instead of an enthusiastic response in the affirmative, they would respond with a litany of things that needed to change before they would invite their friends to church.

If our own congregation was unwilling to invite their unchurched friends to church, how in the world would we be able to reach out to the unbelieving community? We had to change the perception of the church from the inside out. We needed to make the people love the church and be proud of being a part of it, imperfect as it always is.

This led us to start with small concrete changes, which John Kotter in his writing, *Leading Change*, refers to as "generating short term wins" (p. 117). This way the congregation would be able to see that there was a new direction and focus as we moved to, once again, make the church relevant in the community. Perception is a hard thing to quantify as it is of a subjective nature. But if we could generate some positive "buzz" for the church, then what was happening would spread quickly, by word of mouth, to reach those who had a negative perception of the church.

We started a campaign to "love the church." In all age levels, from the pulpit to the children's ministry, we taught them about the church and how we can all make concrete efforts to show our love to the church that God loves. It was as simple as ensuring that the church campus was clean. It meant that we cared for the church.

We also needed a "jump start" and nothing builds more excitement than a building project. While fundamentally change comes from within, it was decided that the church needed a "facelift" to visibly show what was happening. Repair and maintenance had not been proactively done—the once beautiful church looked gloomy and aged. So the church embarked on a four-phased, three-year church renovation and improvement project. The Lord provided providentially and the church never incurred debt. The renovation project brought great pride and excitement to the church members as literally every inch of the church was renovated. It took about three years for the church people to begin to really love the church and perceive their church as a place where they could invite their friends.

The next order of business was to change the perception of those on the outside towards the church. The renovated and modernized facilities sparked the interest of the community. There were some who wanted to come and see the transformed church. The buzz generated was that "something new is happening at Grace Christian Church."

One of the benefits of being associated with a school—and having the school right across the street—was an amazing ministry opportunity to work with the school. However, with that close association comes a close perception. Many graduates could not distinguish "Grace the school" from "Grace the church." If they didn't like the school, then, by association, they didn't like the church either.

Therefore, the first thing we needed to do was to find ways to communicate the distinction between the school and the church. It seemed like a website would be a great starting place. A website would establish not only a presence in cyberspace but would also imply that the church was relevant. While a website is so easy to accomplish, it had never been done. So a website was put up at www.gccp.org.ph. Such a simple change began to transform the outside perception of our church.

Two other methods we utilized to improve our visibility were the social media—such as Facebook and Twitter—and bumper stickers/colorful rubber bracelets—simple marketing techniques. We wanted to let the Chinese community know that there were many people already attending Grace Christian Church and that they were just as welcome to attend. After challenging the congregation to show their love for their church by putting the car stickers on their bumpers—and for the youth to wear the bracelets—the morale of the church members increased, along with a new level of awareness for the larger regional community.

One important fundamental change was instead of planning church events for *only* the church, we would plan church-wide events for the community. Events such as our now annual community fair were held. Whenever we planned an event, we always asked ourselves, "How do we engage and impact the community?" People who had never stepped a foot into the church began to give church a try.

Change #4: We are ONE church
One of the biggest fears of the older generation was that the young

people would change everything and they would find themselves irrelevant and eased out of the church. I have seen it too often: in the desire for a church to be more relevant and cater to the young people, they start a youth service. In an ethnic church, this is manifested through the starting of an English-language service. While there are merits to these decisions, what often happens is that these age-specific and language-specific services can inadvertently create a division inside the church. Each service becomes its own "kingdom," with its own interests.

Being in a culture that prides itself on the importance of family, there were some basic ground rules that we wanted to set before we added more worship services. First of all, each service would cater to all levels. There would not be a "youth" service or a "college" service. It was the hope that the entire family would be able to come together and worship the Lord together. The other rule was that each service would be identical to the other services, with the same preacher, message, worship songs, and announcements.

These policies were put in place to ensure that although we desired to be a multi-site, multi-service church, we would still be *one* church. Anyone who had to attend a service outside of their normal worship time would not feel uncomfortable. There was no "main" service. Each worship service—referred to by their start time—was just as important and valued as the other.

Since we wanted to have this one church culture, the older folks had to adjust to the younger and the younger folks had to adjust to the older as it related to multimedia, worship style, etc. We didn't want to swing the pendulum to an extreme, one way or the other, just to make ourselves more relevant. The reality is that young people do grow up. If the church has a culture where we marginalize those who are older—and celebrate everything young—then the youth of today will find themselves being eased out of relevance in the future.

With four services and plans for additional services, we have seen this model work. Each service is multigenerational. Nothing makes me happier than to see grandparents, parents, teenagers, and children come and worship the Lord together. The one church mentality ingrained within our DNA would ensure that everyone looked out for the good of the church, as opposed to their own personal needs.

Change #5: Church for the Spiritually Broken

Generally speaking, regardless of how a church tries to reach out to all types of people, the demographic makeup of the church usually mimics the demographic makeup of the community that surrounds it. Chinese-Filipino churches tend to be destination churches because there are so few of them in Metro Manila. They become cultural community gathering places. The makeup of the Chinese churches in the Philippines tends to be those in the middle, upper-middle, to the high class of society. This is mentioned because, coupled with a shame-based culture, this makes it hard to reach out to those who are hurting or spiritually broken.

If someone has made a mistake, made wrong choices in life, or has a questionable past, they will no longer attend or look for a Chinese church because of the perceived notion—right or wrong—that they will be ostracized, not accepted, condemned, and ignored. This had to change. One of our church's early desires was to be a church that was safe for the spiritually broken. Our very name implies that we should be a place of grace. While conservative in theology and practice, that doesn't mean we cannot have a culture of welcome, grace, and mercy.

It had to start from the top. The notion of a Chinese church being a place for perfect people probably came about because many of the older generation Chinese pastors preached as if their families were "perfect." Although generalizing about the Chinese pastors' sermons, it seems like many of the principles and virtues taught from the pulpit were reflections from the lives of the pastor's family. However, the reality was that the pastor's family was not perfect, a truth I know having myself grown up in a pastor's family. We had many of the same problems and struggles that every other family went through.

I decided to talk about my brokenness and struggles with the Christian life in my sermons. I was as transparent, real, and normal as I could be. I thought perhaps this would connect with the younger generation since the twenty-first century is a generation that can smell hypocrisy a mile away. But to my surprise, it was the older generation that sent me notes of appreciation for "being real" and authentic. Slowly this began to change the culture of the church—we began to accept people who were broken.

In fact, to our surprise, never before in the history of the church have we had more broken people than we do today. Praise the Lord for that! We have many single parents, wives and children of first and second families attending together. In the Chinese-Filipino community, because there is no divorce allowed in the Philippines, the wife from the first family is the legal wife. Unfortunately, many men have acknowledged mistresses with whom they have a family as well. They are often referred to as the second family.

We even have pastors, after leaving their ministry because of hurts, attending our church as a place of safety. You know you have turned the corner on the cultural attitude toward brokenness when you have ex-pastors attending your church to "hide" between ministries. A typical Chinese church is not a place to "hide."

Change #6: It's Not About the Money

What turns away many people from the church, especially Chinese churches, is the perception that all the church wants is their money. While it is of utmost importance to teach the church about tithing and giving back to the Lord, churches often overemphasize giving and money.

I remember this illustration: The pastor stood before the congregation and said, "I have bad news. I have good news. And I have more bad news." The congregation got quiet. "The bad news is: the church needs a new roof!" The congregation groaned. "The good news is: we have enough money for the new roof." A sigh of relief was heard rippling through the gathered group. "The bad news is: it's still in your pockets!"

But Chinese churches in the Philippines are even worse at times. I know of a situation where a new believer, who didn't have very much, gave all that she had—20 pesos (50 U.S. cents) into the offering plate. The next Sunday, the Chinese pastor chided the congregation saying, "Some of you are scrimping with regard to giving. One of you dared to give God only 20 pesos." The believer was hurt and greatly offended. She vowed she would never go to a Chinese church again. Some time later she was invited to our church. She said she wanted to come because something was different about this church. The church wasn't about the money.

When I accepted the call from the church to be the senior

pastor, the church was going through a difficult time financially. Offering was way down and we could not even pay our utility bills. It would have been easy to spend the first few sermons talking and teaching about giving. However, perhaps in the naivety and idealization of a young pastor, I told the church board that we would trust God for His provision. I told them that if the people are spiritually blessed, convicted, and challenged, they would give.

Long story short, to go from the brink of bankruptcy one year and, in five years' time, embark and complete debt-free a 40 million peso (one million U.S. dollars) renovation—and still be at the best financial position in the forty-five year history of the church—is a testimony to God's provision.

So we changed the culture of the church to one that doesn't focus on the money. We moved from a system of "passing the plate" to an "offering drop box system." While there are benefits to and arguments for both systems, we felt that, for our cultural context and the community we are reaching out to, we wanted to ensure that when people came, they wouldn't feel awkward or obligated to give.

Change #7: Using Change to Teach

As the church grew accustomed to new initiatives, we intentionally infused healthy change as part of the culture of our church. But we didn't simply change for change's sake. We found out that change was a great teaching opportunity. But this can only be done if the church has established "wins" with the changes already proposed.

John Kotter, in his book *Leading Change* writes, "Culture changes only after you have successfully altered people's actions, after the new behavior produces some group benefit for a period of time, and after people see the connection between the new action and the performance improvement" (p. 156).

This should be a word of caution for leaders who want to immediately infuse change as a part of their church's culture. But once it is a part of the culture, one can use change to teach. Let me give an example.

Our church traditionally celebrated communion on the first Sunday of the month, as do many churches. This has been the church pattern for decades. In fact, many people only came to church on the first Sunday of each month to partake in communion. Perhaps because of their Roman Catholic backgrounds, they viewed this ordinance as a sacrament which they needed to do.

One Communion Sunday, I decided that we should not have communion. Many were simply going through the motions. Communion became a dead ritual rather than a wonderful time of self-examination and recommitment. We didn't give any advance notice of this change. We didn't mention during the service that we would make it up the next Sunday or the reason why we didn't have communion.

I cannot tell you how many angry notes I received that week! What a great teaching moment. The next Sunday, I explained to them what our church believes about our celebration of the Lord's Supper. So many people's misconceptions about the practice of communion were corrected. Of course we went back to having it on the first of every month. But every so often we would put it on a different Sunday, just to make sure that people were not coming only for the ritual communion but coming for corporate worship.

I could give countless other examples of how one can use change as teaching moments. May God grant you wisdom, discernment, and grace to know when to use change to teach.

Change in the Church's DNA

By the grace of God, change is now woven into the culture of our church. In a little over eight years, because of the changes that have occurred in our church, and by the grace of God, we have grown from 400 adults and children to over 1,700. While this is not phenomenal growth based on American standards, for a Chinese church in the Philippines this is tremendous growth.

For a culture that is deeply adverse to change, it is wonderful that our church can serve as an example and encouragement to others, illustrating that culture and change are not mutually exclusive. It is our hope that other churches will find encouragement to bravely institute the changes necessary, with truth and love, and with the leading of the Lord, to make an impact in their respective communities.

Jesus came into the world to radically change conventional wisdom—why, then, can our churches not change to meet the needs of an ever-changing environment?

LEADERSHIP UNDER FIRE
Resolving Personal Conflict in a High Pressure World
Suzanne Martinez

One of the most exhilarating and challenging times in my life and career was when I stepped into the role as a lead manager for a Fortune 100 company.

For most of those thirteen years, I was engaged in various types of Department of Defense Contracts at the Pentagon. Some seasons were stretching, but there was a two and half year period when I experienced intense leadership situations. During that time we were supporting a major military command in its nationwide soldier training and readiness activities.

Many of the lessons learned during those years were instrumental in helping me be more effective in my future local church ministry. Whether you are on staff in a formal ministry, are bi-vocational or fully engaged in the marketplace, I pray that my story might help you lead well during your own times of leadership crisis.

Into the Fire

During my tenure, our account grew from less than 25 people with almost no business to over 300 people with $65 million per year.

The work demanded managing operations, responding to rapid change, working with senior-level clients—including generals, handling classified to top secret information, and troubleshooting daily crises, whether related to personnel or technical issues.

My temperament and gifting are stimulated by great challenge and include a willingness to assume responsibility for all aspects of issues. Because of those orientations, I was often drawn to two types of scenarios—situations that were either brand-new, start-up enterprises, or messy, conflicted situations that needed turning around—or sometimes a combination of both.

This major command's work included a combination of both. The two managers who hired me were visionaries—optimistic and enthusiastic men full of more ideas than they possibly could have implemented on their own. They needed a leader who was a possibility thinker and an optimist, one who could carry their ideas to fruition and accomplish the mission.

Initially, they hired me into an ambiguous role, without a title or anything in particular communicated to me or the team regarding my responsibilities. This is not unusual in either rapidly growing corporations or churches, due to the intensity of the growth and the temperaments and tendencies of entrepreneurial leaders.

In retrospect, the reason I was willing to accept such an ambiguous role was the chemistry and connection I felt with the two men, as well as an intuitive sense that what they needed was a good fit for my skill set. That trial period also gave me an opportunity to work with the team and a chance for them to become accustomed to me as the account leader.

Within a few weeks, one of the two men asked me to assume the official title and position of the deputy program manager. He, the team and I had developed a great working relationship and moved forward with enthusiasm into this new organizational structure.

Within a short time, perhaps weeks, he transferred the program manager leadership role over to me completely, saying, "You're so much better at this than me … I'm going to go do business development." I wasn't so sure about the reasoning, but he went on and found much fulfillment in his new role.

Little did I realize the formidable challenges that laid in store with that quick transition—that these leaders' willingness to be ambiguous and rapid regarding transition would manifest itself again, in a way that would be painful.

Unlike my leaders, perhaps God led me to this position to teach me about handling intense leadership challenges. He planned to teach me how to handle dynamic, ongoing conflict, to maintain strong boundaries and limits amidst massive workloads, to fully rely on Him to sustain me, and to prepare me for future leadership roles. God also planned to test and grow my boundaries. The leadership challenges I faced not only stretched my leadership boundaries, but also my personal, emotional, and sexual boundaries.

The Furnace Heats Up

A difficult test of my leadership boundaries included the addition to our team of an older leader from within our company, a transfer which I did not have an opportunity to approve. This leader, like many of the men on my team, was perhaps a couple of decades older than me. While the rest of the team worked well, it became apparent early on that reporting to me offended this gentleman's sensibilities.

He demonstrated that he would not submit to me or the authority of my position as program manager. He attempted to undermine me by taking over meetings with counter-proposals or simply showing his lack of respect for my authority through his body language during program meetings with the client and team.

Initially, my two leaders supported me, letting him know where the door was if he couldn't learn to play on the team. Looking back, it would have been helpful to fire this man from the team early on. Yet, because I had not hired him, I sensed I would not have full support to transfer him. Although I confronted each incident with grace and patience, he was a disruption to me and the team. A subsequent restructure helped matters; over time we developed a constructive working relationship.

Additional tests of my boundaries included intense conflicts that were a daily part of my position. Not only were there intra-team conflicts, but there were conflicts with clients and competitor companies. An ongoing situation involved a major client, the civilian contract manager, with whom I worked closely. This person was a rageaholic and extremely difficult to satisfy. In one instance, this client screamed at me at the front desk over a situation we were working to resolve—in front of a potential new employee and an administrative assistant. I had to rely on the Lord to exercise self-control and poise, responding to her with grace and diplomacy.

In another instance, this client, my manager and I were

in her office to deal with a problem that had arisen. She screamed at my manager; I was stunned and felt humiliated for him. He did not respond to her anger and seemed to freeze in response, which shocked me.

Somewhere along the line, I learned that men shut down their emotions when they are angry in an attempt to avoid hurting people—either verbally or otherwise. Looking back, I'm certain that's why he responded as he did to her disrespectful behavior. This man was a good leader, and her disrespect to him was inappropriate and unprofessional.

This leader was not the only volatile member of this major command; another female used sarcasm, contempt, and intimidation when working with leaders—whether male or female, contractors or team members. These female leaders apparently knew little of how to motivate people—especially men—nor knew how to elicit cooperation from them for the mission at hand.

In the situation with the raging clients, Scripture would say to exercise the fruit of self-control and gentleness with these people. Proverbs 15:1 tells us that a harsh word stirs up anger, but a gentle answer soothes wrath. Galatians 5:22-23 adds that gentleness and self-control are vital character qualities, only possible to exhibit as we walk in the Spirit (Gal. 5:25).

There were many other intense and difficult personalities, some in the leadership of my corporation and others on my teams. God provided plenty of opportunities for me to walk in the Spirit, despite the intense pressure and the volatile personalities involved.

Managing Conflict in the Fire

The ongoing conflict began to wear on me, as it can on any leader when conflicts are constant and chronic. The situation with the raging client continued to be problematic with her ill-timed blow-ups. A manager friend suggested I go to lunch with her or do other steps to build the relationship. I resisted his suggestions—they seemed disingenuous and political. This manager anticipated my objections, asserting that he thought his suggestions would help.

The nuggets of wisdom I missed in his counsel were the

two strategies of: 1) stepping out of my task-oriented, "get-things-done" mode, and 2) leaning into her aggressive behavior, rather than withdrawing from her.

My superiors had always praised me for my ability to resolve conflict. They nicknamed me the "velvet hammer" because of my ability to get difficulties resolved without much fallout, leaving people feeling positive. They would often joke, saying, "Shall we send in our hammer to work out this situation?" Yet, at a later point, one of these same leaders accused me of taking a "bunker mentality." Even though his criticism was harsh, it made me realize that I needed to grow in my abilities, becoming more proactive in resolving conflicts—conflicts that seemed to go out of control quickly in our high-pressure environment.

Matthew 18:15 teaches us to confront those who offend us one-on-one, giving them the opportunity to hear our concern and change their actions and attitudes. It goes on to say that if they hear us and change, then we have won them over. Often, however, with severe or longstanding conflicts, people will not be won over in one meeting. The subsequent verses, 16-17, provide the strategy for when the one-on-one strategy fails; return to the person with one or two witnesses to again try to resolve the conflict.

If that strategy fails, we are to "take it to the church," meaning not necessarily the person's entire church, but their spiritual accountability system. That could include their pastors, small group, or a group of spiritual friends to whom they might listen. Scripture adds that if all of these strategies fail, then treat the person as an unbeliever, as they have refused to submit to God's Word or His people's admonitions. This ostracism is done in the hope that the loss of fellowship, in conjunction with the Spirit's continued work, might bring about conviction for their sin and genuine repentance on their behalf.

God gave me many opportunities to grow in my abilities to resolve conflict, practice these principles in the marketplace setting, and trust Him in the midst of these conflicts.

Trusting God in the Fire

Another significant instance included a surprise reorganization. Because of a combination of factors, including our need to have a more regular presence at the command's operational center, the decision was made to split the team and have me lead the half that would be at the command's center.

The reorganization was shocking as I had not been consulted during its planning. I felt betrayed. An insider let me know that a new manager had been transferred in from our corporate site, even though she lacked the required leadership or client experience.

This transfer was due in part to political reasons, perhaps a favor owed to someone on the home site leadership chain. My core leadership team had dissolved without any warning. It took a number of months for me to recover from that blow and regain a measure of trust in the leadership.

Some months later, a manager who worked for me submitted a surprise resignation. This manager had worked for and with me for years and was a close friend. He rescinded his resignation the next day, but it was too late.

I knew that for him to even consider resigning, there must have been breaches of trust in our relationship. Because of our friendship and his importance to the contract, I allowed him to stay in his role. But that final breach of trust cut deeply and caused me to be on guard with him.

Betrayal in the Fire

For most leaders, betrayal in leadership is the most difficult experience they will face. This betrayal of my leaders and this manager, with whom I believed I had close and trusting relationships, seemed more severe because of old wounds.

There are psychological triggers that we experience when similar situations bring forth exacerbated, emotional reactions due to past life events. The reorganization and resignation triggered past, hurtful experiences for me, causing me to react more strongly than it would seem the situations warranted. It's important for leaders to be aware of their triggers to guard against overreacting to developments in their leadership and lives.

Scripture records that Jesus was betrayed by Peter, with whom He had a personal relationship—the betrayal being caused by Peter's fear. Jesus was also betrayed by Judas, who didn't really care about Christ but wanted to use Him for his own selfish purposes. As leaders, we can be betrayed by those with whom we are close, and those who want to use us for their own selfish motivations. Either way, betrayal is extremely painful.

The primary comfort I found within that experience was knowing that in Christ I was appreciated, loved and accepted—not because of my performance, but because of my person. Throughout that painful season, I trusted and prayed that Christ would vindicate my work. I knew I had worked hard to give my best to Him and the team.

After the reorganization, I transferred to the command center to see what God had planned. I felt a little like Joseph on the way to prison. Yet God was gracious and continued to bless my work with the new team. Before long, we were given another $9M of work. The same leader who had engineered the reorganization was amazed, asking how we continued to get so much new work. I knew God was blessing the work as I committed it to Him daily, determining to be a positive witness.

I always viewed my position as an evangelistic one. Because of my leadership role, I was not permitted to share the gospel openly. However, I could lead by example and with integrity. Everyone with whom I worked—clients, competitors, and team members—knew that I was a Christian. I could intercede for them through prayer, whether or not they realized it, and for the situations in which we found ourselves.

Exercising Self-Control and Boundaries in the Fire

Boundaries at the major command center continued to be a challenge, not only with the long hours and what seemed to be a never-ending workload, but also with the attentions I received from various command personnel. As I worked to build good relationships, I tried to be friendly and positive. Yet I had learned from my years at the Pentagon to be careful in how I interacted with men, including civilians, military clients, and team members.

One lieutenant colonel began to show significant interest in me, coming by my office often to talk and offering to help me with my bags or walk me to the parking garage when I worked late. Since this gentleman was married, I knew to be concerned about the attention I was receiving from him. The man even offered to take me to the airport late one evening when I was traveling out-of-town. When a manager friend heard about it, he asked, "Is he going to get out of bed with his wife to take you to the airport?" We agreed that this wasn't appropriate and I assured him I'd take a cab or have a friend drive me to the airport instead.

There were occasional, out-of-state trips for conferences. During one of these trips, I saw a high-level leader coming out of the hotel room of a senior-level leader one morning. I was disgusted, although my co-worker appeared nonplussed, saying, "Come on, Suzanne, you know this stuff is going on." After working so hard over the years to be a godly and honorable leader who operated with integrity, this was especially hard for me to stomach.

There were also attractive people on our contract who created regular tests of my emotional boundaries and self-control. I recall one man with whom I worked closely. Whenever I met with him in his office, I would look at the pictures of his wife and children and remind myself that I would never do anything to damage his family or disgrace my Lord. Although he was an ongoing temptation, God gave me continual victory as I prayed for self-control, talked with a close girlfriend for accountability and prayer, and worked hard to stay out of compromising situations involving him. Nothing untoward ever took place between the two of us during all the years we worked together. I am grateful that we conducted ourselves in a way that we have no regrets.

In the situation with the attractive leader, Scripture reveals the key to victory is to exercise self-control through the power of the Holy Spirit. The Spirit gave me a check if I moved near any type of danger zone. Scripture warns us that in the two areas of immorality and idolatry, we are to always "flee" from temptation, rather than attempt to resist it, because these two sins are so powerful in their draw on us. Because I heeded Scripture's warnings and held myself accountable, God enabled me to achieve victory over these strong temptations.

Another time that I had to practice self-control was with my workload. At the command center, the competition was becoming more and more intense as we were competing for a new contract. The hours and workload became more challenging and a daily fire-hose of problems kept coming at me. I often worked through lunch, stopping at about 3:00 p.m. for a quick salad to keep my energy levels up for the long evening hours ahead.

After one day in which I had worked fourteen hours—and was exhausted after many months of such a schedule—my best friend and prayer partner chastised me, reminding me I couldn't be responsible for everything, no matter how hard I worked. She urged me to step back and pace myself in order to avoid burnout.

This was difficult. My tendencies to lead, manage, and show strong responsibility for whatever is entrusted to me—whether at work, home, or in friendships—were hard to rein in. Even my parental leadership models were similar. My dad was up as early as 4:00 a.m. as a farmer and waterman, often working into the night. My mom was also a hard and responsible worker. I am the oldest child so I have carried much responsibility at home since my childhood. During this season of life, I was unmarried and without children, so it was easy to become consumed with the mission of the work. A saving grace for me during that time were seminary courses I had been taking, in the hopes that God would someday open a full-time ministry path for me. Another saving grace was a volunteer ministry I was involved with at my church. These two diversions were critical to help me keep my life in balance, a balance that felt precarious at times.

In Ecclesiastes 2:17-23, Solomon reflected on the meaninglessness of toil, and even great achievements, which he concluded only led to grief, pain, and a restless mind. He added in verse 26 that God gives wisdom, knowledge and happiness to those who please Him. The psalmist further added in Psalm 127:2 that it is vain to arise early and stay up late, because the Lord grants sleep to those He loves.

Overwork can be the bane of the "Type-A" personality, particularly if they are working to shore up a performance-based self-image. Because I was blessed to come to Christ as a child, I knew my worth was in Christ. But in a performance-based leadership culture, it is an ongoing discipline for Christian leaders to remember that their worth is in Christ, not in how others evaluate their work. Leaders also need to remember the importance of rest and balance in their lives, being accountable to others to maintain a healthy work and life balance.

God's Work Accomplished through the Fire

Through each challenge, God showed Himself faithful by continually blessing me in these leadership roles. No matter what circumstance seemed to be thrown my way, God worked it for good. He enabled me to build a business and team that brought millions of dollars into our company coffers, while simultaneously developing hundreds of leaders in their own career paths. God used this amazing season in my career to develop me as a leader and prepare me for full-time vocational ministry.

While serving as the full-time program manager at the command center, I was simultaneously serving part-time as the director of the 30's-40's singles ministry at my church. After serving in that position for two years, God led me to leave my marketplace position to serve full-time in ministry.

This ministry role required serving thousands of people, overseeing multiple staff with large budgets, and dealing with the never-ending demands on my time and energy. The memories of God's amazing provisions while at the Pentagon and the command center were fresh in my mind as we faced mountains of work and challenges at the church.

God had prepared me well for the challenges in ministry. I was grateful and humbled by the opportunity to serve Him in His church.

Lessons Learned in the Fire

Throughout the two and a half years at the command center, God taught me several lessons. Each of the lessons involved various aspects of walking in integrity amidst temptations in many areas of my life.

- God helped me grow in my character in the fruit of self-control. He taught me to exercise self-control in the midst of people's volatile emotions, most often anger and rage, and to refuse to allow myself to be controlled by someone else's lack of control.

- God taught me about boundaries and overwork—reinforcing what I had known intellectually but now learned experientially—that my work performance does not equate to my worth.

- God taught me about boundaries and sexual temptation. I learned that staying accountable, praying for strength, fleeing from compromising situations, and relying on the Holy Spirit would give me spiritual and emotional victory amidst the fiery dangers of sexual and emotional temptations.

- God taught me that though I am loyal in relationships, others will betray and disappoint me, often deeply. God is the only One who will never betray me, even if His will disappoints or confuses me. I learned experientially the truth of Romans 12:2—that as my mind was renewed, I would experience that His will is always "good, pleasing, and perfect."

- Lastly, God taught me to deeply trust His sovereignty, His control, and His resources, rather than my own. Every surprising and painful obstacle I encountered had been His way of growing my character in godliness. For that I am thankful and grateful.

HELP, I NEED SOMEBODY!
How I Learned to Hire Staff
Raymond Y. Chang

John was an incredibly gifted, intelligent and capable leader. His résumé was everything we had hoped for in our most critical position, the Pastor of Inreach. This position oversaw the areas of new visitor assimilation, small group leadership development and overall spiritual growth catalyst. In a growing church, this was the core ministry of our church.

In a relatively new church plant, we were evolving from a single pastor to a multi-staff organism. We contacted our immediate social network and asked two questions: "If you were to hire someone, who would you hire?" and, "Do you know of anyone available that would fit this position?"

Like most churches, after we followed the typical path of personal networking, asking pastoral friends if they knew anyone who would be the right person for this position, we went to our trusted seminary job placement director who then sent us a packet of résumés. Finally, we looked at internet ministry job sites and posted our ministry need.

After this three-step gathering process, we saw John's résumé in the pile given to us by one of the seminaries. John's résumé was one of the few impressive résumés sorted to the possible candidates pile. He made the first cut.

What impressed us about John was his academic credentials. Since we both graduated from the same seminary, I knew that his theological framework would be similar to mine. He was completing a doctoral degree from a prestigious overseas university and was ready and wanting to move into a pastoral position.

Of course, with any résumé there are strengths and

weaknesses. For John, his strength was his academics. His weakness was his lack of experience. As a young church with a young pastoral team—serving a congregation of highly educated professionals—we thought John would be a good fit for our church.

So we began the interview process with John. We first scheduled an interview using an internet video conference call. In our initial conversation, we discussed his training, his passion and his vision for ministry. So far everything seemed like a good fit to move forward with him in our search process.

Then we took the next step of bringing John out for a personal interview for a weekend. The weekend was packed with interviews with various teams he would be leading. Our goal was simply to measure chemistry with the people he would be working with and serving alongside.

Last, we had him meet with the board. This is where we began to sense that John's lack of experience would become a major issue. While John was academically well-read, his lack of practical knowledge of how ministry actually worked began to raise some red flags. He presented a flowchart of how he was going to *change* our whole small group structure. The flowchart looked great on paper but was all theory, without practical value.

Through the weekend, we began to realize his lack of experience was going to play a major role; however, we wanted to give John the benefit of the doubt. We reasoned that he could learn whether his ideas would work or not through the school of hard knocks.

But another issue surfaced when we spoke to his references— his friends and former employers. Through these conversations, we began to notice a pattern. John was a hard worker but liked to work by himself. He loved to study. He loved teaching. However, nobody commented about his pastoral skills. One reference even mentioned he should be in an academic teaching context and not in a church.

Even with this caution, we liked John's desire to serve on a pastoral team and his willingness to come to our church. John seemed like a good fit and we would try to help John learn most of these skills on the job.

Even though we began to see some major issues, we were enamored with John's résumé and his potential. We offered John the position and, a few months later, John arrived at our church. John lasted a little over a year and then left the pastoral team to become a professor at a nearby college. While we celebrated John's journey of finding the right fit for his gifts, the church was back to square one, just as it was a year earlier, looking for the right staff person.

Finding the Right Person

Finding the right associate staff is one of the most critical decisions a church can make. Often, finding the wrong person with the wrong fit can bring crises or set a ministry back. For some, this can become a source of conflict and dissension. When John left our church, we were happy for him; however, we realized that ministry took two steps back when we had to start over.

In one employment article, the authors made the obvious comment regarding the setback of hiring new employees. They write:

> According to the Studer Group, 'A survey of 610 CEOs by Harvard Business School estimates that typical mid-level managers require 6.2 months to reach their break-even point.' Bliss breaks down the productivity scale into three periods: during the first month or so, after training is completed, new employees are functioning at about 25% productivity, which means that the cost of lost productivity is 75% of the employee's salary. The level goes up to 50% productivity for weeks 5 through 12, with corresponding cost of 50% of employee salary. Weeks 13 through 20 usually bring the employee up to 75% productivity rate, with the cost being 25% of employee salary. Around the five-month mark, then, companies can expect a new hire to reach full productivity.

Loss of money, time and relational investment is detrimental to the growth of any ministry. Sadly, like most ministry lessons, we learned the hard way in hiring the right person with the right fit.

On the corollary, finding the right person can also propel the ministry forward. In a *Ministry Today* magazine article, "Help! My Church Won't Grow," the author asks, "Who comprises the staff? This includes both paid and volunteer. A church will rarely grow beyond the capacity of its staff. One of the easiest, surest ways to foster church growth is to add people with staff responsibilities (not necessarily salary). The benefit to each of those new 'staff members' and to the whole church cannot be overstated."

In many ways, finding the right staff is similar to finding a marriage partner. Dating can be a fun experience but when you make a commitment, you have to seriously consider multiple factors.

In the next section are some practical lessons that we learned through the process of staff transition. In the past ten years, we have hired thirty paid staff positions including full-time, part-time and independent contractors.

Here is a simple paradigm to evaluate staff. Included are three critical prerequisites to any staff hire. Following the prerequisites are five areas to evaluate.

Three Prerequisites: Assessment, Experience, and References

1) Proper Assessment

One of the core passions at our church is church planting. Finding the right planter begins with having the correct assessment. Not everyone is wired to be a church planter. It takes a unique gift mix to be an effective church planter. The key is to do the right assessment. In the same way, having a comprehensive assessment is critical.

Since most churches may not have a comprehensive assessment process, it is important to set up a simple assessment system. Assessment is simply looking at and measuring how the person is gifted and wired. There are formal organizations that do assessments for individuals. However, a simple assessment consists of a spiritual gifts inventory, a psychological profile and determining the leadership style.

First, the candidate should go through a simple assessment process with measurement tools like DiSC, MBTI, a spiritual gifts inventory and StrengthsFinder. Second, they should go through a behavioral interview, which is simply an interview that looks on past performance. In most behavioral interviews, the key emphasis is "past performance measures future success."

The goal is to a get a broad picture of who the candidate is rather than who we think the candidate should be. So often we have an image formed of the person—we have to recognize that the person is wired by God to be a certain way. This is how leaders are made. I agree with Robert Clinton in his book, *The Making of a Leader*:

> The major work is that which God is doing to and in the (young) leader, not through him or her. Most emerging leaders don't recognize this. They evaluate productivity, activities, fruitfulness, etc. But God is quietly, often in unusual ways, trying to get the leader to see that one ministers out of what one is. God is concerned with what we are. We want to learn a thousand things to do. But He will teach us one thing, perhaps in a thousand ways: 'I am forming Christ in you.' It is this that will give power to your ministry.

Assessment is simply asking the question, "How did God form this individual and how is God forming them for His purpose?" One final word of wisdom: make sure there are several people assessing the individual. Getting more people involved in the process will bring better discernment. Proverbs 15:22 reminds us, "Plans fail for lack of counsel, but with many advisers they succeed."

2) Evaluate Experience

The next step in any candidate selection is to correctly evaluate their past experience. Looking back at the beginning of the chapter, we realized that John didn't have any experience. We hired him for the position knowing he would learn through experience.

We needed to make sure the experience was comparable to his role. In other words, just because someone has experience leading small groups doesn't automatically translate into successful small group leading at our church. There are multiple factors in determining whether experience is helpful in this process.

For example, if your ministry is looking for an operations person but the candidate only has a decade of pastoral experience and seminary training, it may not necessarily mean this person will be a good fit for the role.

Recently, we were in the process of hiring a pastor of ministry operations. Similar to an executive pastor, this person would oversee budget, staff hiring, board management, and ministry systems development. The person we would hire would be someone with a high organizational background.

We had two candidates. One was a young man who had fifteen years of pastoral experience—not highly administrative, but a great pastoral heart with strong relational gifts. Second, we had a candidate with no pastoral experience. However, he oversaw a million dollar budget as the director of an extension campus of a local Christian university.

As we evaluated the position, we realized that because this role was more administrative and organizational, the type of experience required was administrative rather than pastoral. Even though this campus director had a seminary background, he never served on a pastoral team. However, his gifts were better suited than the candidate who had pastoral experience yet a limited administrative background.

3) Seek References

The third prerequisite in the search process is making sure you have the proper references. The general rule of references is that if the candidate puts the reference on his résumé, the reference will probably only have good things to say about the candidate.

Here are some ways we try to use the references. First, we ask two simple questions: "What do you see as the candidate's primary strengths?" and, "What do you see as the candidate's primary areas of growth?" With both questions, our goal is to simply get a consistent theme.

After getting the references, we always try to find references that might not be the first layer of references, but also a second or third layer. This might be done by asking the first group of references if they know of any other people who know the candidate. Our desire is to simply get a well-rounded, outside perspective.

Sometimes the types of references a candidate puts on their résumé can be an indicator of what type of candidate this person might be. As one educational search firm, SJG (The Spelman and Johnson Group) writes to potential candidates:

Having another professional speak on your behalf as a reference is an important and critical part of a job search and should be managed with utmost care. All too often candidates simply submit a list of references and consider that aspect of the process complete. As a candidate, this laissez faire response to providing references will no longer serve you effectively in your job search process. Instead, you should think carefully about whom you ask to speak on your behalf, what a particular reference will be able to speak to in terms of your skills and experiences as a candidate, and if a potential reference can speak articulately to what makes you a strong candidate for the position.

With these three prerequisites, it's time to move to our five primary areas of evaluation, areas that need to be considered for the right fit. Of course, there is no such thing as a "perfect" fit but we are looking for the "best fit." One key principle to keep in mind is to look for potential as much as the actual. For the sake of simplicity, I will use the letter "C" for each of these ideas.

Five Core Areas of Evaluation

If we are making a checklist of important qualifications, the first one would be *calling*. For any Christian leader, the first question has to be "Why?" Calling is at the heart of why we do ministry. Asking the question why we do what we do drives at the heart of motivation. Then from calling flows out *character*. Character defines who we really are; it is our core identity. Then from character, we have to examine the skill set. This would be defined as *competency*. Next, with character and competency, which focuses on the candidate, the ministry must also match the person with the organizational *culture and context*. This is the question of values. Finally, the last area is the most subjective and yet it can be the most important. Does this person have the right *chemistry* to mix with our church?

More than a completely objective checklist, this serves as a grid, a guideline to help make a wise choice. Let's explore each one.

1. Calling: Why am I doing this?

The first question is a clear sense of call to ministry and to this position. Calling is something we see from a general sense where God calls all men to salvation (Rom. 8:30; 1 Cor. 1:9, 1 Thes. 2:12). But in a specific sense, God calls people to specific ministries. This could be for a season or for a lifetime. Throughout the Scriptures, we see specific people who are "called out" for a special purpose. Abram was called out of Ur to an unknown land. Moses was called out of Egypt to lead the people of Israel toward the promised land. David was called out to be the king to govern the people. Even in the New Testament, we see Jesus calling the disciples to follow Him and lead others. Of course, the most classic example of calling was Paul, who was called on the road to Damascus.

Throughout church history, there are men and women who are called for specific tasks and ministries. Related with the idea of calling is also spiritual calling. Those whom God calls, He also equips for the work of ministry (Eph. 4:12).

Asking the question of calling is really asking the question of motivation. Why are we doing what we are doing? Knowing that God has a specific task for me to fulfill can be a source of strength, especially during times of difficulty in ministry.

2. Character: Who am I?

Someone once defined character as "who you are when nobody is looking." It is who we are at the core of our being. It's our integrity, humility, faithfulness, joy, peace, love, and, most importantly, our godliness. It's our values. It's the thing that defines our identity. One challenge of evaluating character is that it is hard to measure in an interview. If you ever asked a candidate if they lacked character, I doubt anyone would answer that they have no character. Yet, we all know of individuals that were hired and then, through their actions, we realized that they displayed a lack of patience, kindness, self-control, etc.

In one report and character assessment test, it was discovered that the causes of turnover are primarily due to some character dysfunction:

- 60% is due to some form of relational fracture

with a boss or peer or a character dysfunction that is manifested in poor performance or behavior.
- 20% is related to the candidate's expectations not being met.
- 10% is from failure to perform the skill a person was hired for.
- 10% is uncontrollable due to changes in personal circumstances.

How does a ministry safeguard the character issue? For one, references can be helpful if you know *who* to ask. Generally, most references would be positive about a person's character. Rarely would a candidate put a reference on their résumé who disparaged their character. Rather, we would ask the candidate to supply references of people who worked with them and under them. Then we would go another layer by asking those references if they knew of other references. This would ensure a 360 approach (supervisor, coworker and subordinate) reference check.

In addition, there are some character and personality tools like the DiSC profile, Myers-Briggs and the MERIT profile. There are numerous other tools that can be used to give a glimpse behind the scenes of someone's character.

But the character challenge is more than just past behavior—it is also our core beliefs and values. Asking a good set of questions can be a helpful way to discern character issues and problems. For example, asking an open-ended case study question can be a good approach. Ask yourself what kind of character you want the person to possess and then ask what kind of issues might happen in your context.

An open-ended question like, "You are instructed to follow specific instructions on organizing an event. You are given step-by-step instructions. But you feel that you can do it differently and more effectively. What would you do in this case?" Here you have the candidate work through a scenario, measuring how he follows instructions yet also learning how he makes adjustments. Would he just do it his own way, without communication, or would he follow instructions? Open-ended questions can give some reference points to explore some other issues.

Finally, it's important to differentiate between a character flaw and a growth area. We had one candidate who was perpetually disorganized. All his references pointed out that he would start something but never follow through. For some this could be a serious character flaw (laziness, disrespect, pride, etc.) or it could be a growth area. This may be a personality issue where a person has to learn to cope with this weakness. Does this person acknowledge this weakness and that he is willing to deal with this in his ministry? Does this person openly share or does this person conceal? There shouldn't be too many surprises. If he fails to disclose important past behavior that might affect his job, then it could be a good indicator of a character flaw.

3. Competency: What do I do well?

The next item on the checklist is competency—the skills and experience a person brings to the organization and ministry. This is what most résumés focus on. Can they speak, write, lead, play an instrument, organize an event or mobilize people? Competency is simply what they are good at, gifted with or passionate about. In other words, do they have the necessary skills to do their job and do it well?

With calling and character being the foundation of a person, competencies serve as the pillars. Looking at past performance is a good indicator of what he has done well. Also helpful is asking questions about what he enjoys doing and what he is passionate about.

Most competencies can be developed and enhanced. In our ministry, we try to enhance and enlarge people's competencies by providing a "roadmap" or a development plan to increase their areas of competencies. Also, one of the roles an organization can take is to help the individual work on new areas of competencies. The person may never have been given the opportunity to try new areas.

We had one candidate who came in as a worship candidate, having experience from his previous ministries. His musical gifts were exceptional. He had an incredible voice. Throughout our conversation, he expressed a desire to do more counseling and shepherding of people. While his primary gifts and experience were in music, his heart was for pastoring people. After we hired him as a worship leader, he began leading a small group of young adults. Then he began shepherding and counseling people in prayer. Eventually, he moved completely out of the worship role into a pastoral equipping role. This was a person who had competencies beyond what we hired him for. The key for us was to allow him to explore other ministry areas, where he found joy and fulfillment.

4. Culture/Context: Where is my place?
With competencies evaluated, every candidate has to be a good "cultural" fit. This is the fit of the organization to the person. Every ministry has a built-in culture. Often, the church is blind to its own culture and context. Like fish in water, because they are so used to their surroundings, the church assumes everyone will fit into its culture. Sometimes there is an unstated expectation that the candidate already knows and understands how everything works. This is often where culture shock happens with new employees. What works in one context may not necessarily work in the next.

Even if a candidate is the best candidate with the right calling, character and competencies, if this person doesn't fit the church culture, then this could become a bad situation for everyone. As a young pastor, I had the privilege of working at the First Evangelical Free Church of Fullerton. The Senior Pastor was Chuck Swindoll, who eventually became the President of Dallas Theological Seminary and pastor at Stonebriar Community Church near Dallas, Texas.

I learned a valuable lesson from Chuck on the value of the right context. Early in Chuck's ministry, he took a pastorate at a church near Boston, a smaller church with a long history. Chuck, a recent graduate of Dallas Theological Seminary, born and raised in Houston, Texas, was called to this northeastern church. Despite his clear sense of call—and incredible gift to communicate—he lasted in this church for about a year. It was a challenging and difficult ministry. He joked that the best view of the church was the one in the rearview mirror as he was driving away.

He remarked how this was a challenging ministry because the cultural context was so radically different. Expectations were different. Style of ministry was different. Eventually, he came to Southern California and pastored in the city of Fullerton. There he found a great cultural and contextual fit for his gifts. The rest is history.

Ministry context is not only a major factor but is something that a ministry or organization must have clarity about before it hires. Asking questions related to the values of the organization and its expectations will go a long way in finding a better match.

5. Chemistry: How do I play with the rest of the team?
The last item on the checklist is the one of chemistry. One Christian leader, Larry Osborne, a Senior Pastor at North Coast Church in San Diego, reminded young leaders at a conference that chemistry is an essential ingredient to a successful team. He said, "Winning teams deliberately work on chemistry, they don't take it for granted or assume it will happen."

Chemistry is how we "mesh," how we "play," how we "work." This is often something that people or ministries don't focus on. In reality, this can be a tremendous source of stress or satisfaction. Can we work well together? Of course, this doesn't necessarily mean that everyone on the staff are best friends ... but it does mean that everybody works together, with a spirit of camaraderie.

Out of all the checklist items, this is the most subjective. One of the church planting leaders of a denomination once told me his basic criteria for selecting a church planter. He asked one profound question, "Do I like you?" He said that if someone was likable then he would attract people and make the gospel attractive.

I would say this final characteristic is an important one to discuss, finding out how this person works with others. I like how one article writer describes the importance of chemistry in ministry hires. He writes:

> Chemistry is how we connect with others on the team. It is the most subjective of the three; it is far less measurable than character and competence. Chemistry could be described as team fit. Chemistry occurs when members of the same ministry team fit well together; they gel, connect, and synergize.
>
> The longer I am in church leadership, the more I see the value of chemistry in building ministry teams. Jim Collins, author of *Good to Great*, conducted copious research of great companies and discovered that

teamwork is an essential component to their success.

In the book, he writes: 'If we get the right people on the bus, the right people in the right seats, and the wrong people off the bus, then we'll figure out how to take it someplace great.' Great ministry teams have the right people on the bus in the right seats. Building a cohesive team is exceedingly difficult if the chemistry is not present—if the right people are not on the bus.

If the other items are the building blocks of a good staff, chemistry is the glue that binds the other four items on the lists together. A great team will always have great chemistry.

Another Story: One Important Reminder to Pray

At the beginning of this chapter, I shared the story of John. He was a great guy but wasn't a great fit. We ignored the warning signs and bypassed the process. We saw potential but this wasn't the right fit.

Let me share another staff hire. The most important part of the process we often neglect is the importance of prayer throughout the process. While this is not an organizational principle, it is the most important principle for the body of Christ. It is through prayer that we gain wisdom, discernment and faith.

In my first church plant near Washington D.C., our vision was to reach a diverse city with a multi-cultural and multiethnic vision. Even though our church was predominately a young adult church, mostly from Asian American backgrounds, we wanted to find someone who would come from a different background. Someone once told me that not only do we need to state our vision, we also need to "staff" our vision.

Through a contact of a mutual friend, we prayed that God would bring a non-Asian to work with our church. As we prayed for guidance, direction and wisdom, we met a young man who had recently graduated from seminary. Even though he wasn't Asian, he was in a bi-cultural marriage with an Asian wife.

We went through our process of assessment, evaluation, and references. Everything was extremely positive. Then we examined the checklist: he was called to pastor and lead. His character was spoken highly of by others. His competencies were in the area of leadership, counseling and shepherding others. Culturally, while he wasn't of Asian background, he understood the dynamics of working with Asian Americans, as well as working in a diverse background. Finally, we had similar passions for helping others achieve their vision in ministry.

The only concern we had was that he had limited pastoral experience. However, as we prayed, God began to lead us to step out in faith. We wanted to invest in this young leader.

This was the best hire we had made. A year later, I was called out of the church plant back to my home church in Los Angeles. The person who took over my position was Scott Barfoot, the young leader who had joined our staff just a year prior (and also a writer/editor of this book.)

For the past 15 years, Scott has remained one of my closest friends in ministry. The great news about having the right person and the right fit is seeing how God can use the person in the journey. The journey began when the right person joined the right church with the right fit.

A TURNAROUND STORY IN PROGRESS
Crisis for a New Senior Pastor
Caleb Kaltenbach

Valley View Christian Church was poised for significant growth …
until a domino effect of events unraveled everything.

Valley View Christian Church was started in 1964. It has
its roots within the non-denominational Independent Christian
Churches. Their longest standing pastor was there over thirty years.

The church grew from a few people in the beginning to around
1,500 in attendance 36 years later. In the early 2000's, the church
moved from a smaller facility in the town of Farmers Branch to the
city of Dallas. The new building included a 1,500-seat auditorium,
gym, two children's wings, youth worship room, office wing, Sunday
school classrooms, choir room, and coffee room.

Tragically, the senior pastor was diagnosed with Parkinson's
Disease shortly after moving to the new campus. He retired and the
elders promoted the associate pastor to the position of senior pastor.
The new senior pastor had served as a worship pastor and associate
pastor for over 25 years, but never had served as a senior pastor.

During this time, people in the church started to leave. Some
complained that they didn't like the new senior pastor's preaching;
others missed the longstanding pastor. The elders made a decision to
bring in a preaching pastor to lead and preach, along with the senior
pastor.

As one can imagine, this did not go well. Eventually, the senior
pastor left and took a position at a nearby church that former Valley
View Christian Church members had formed. On top of that, the
church split happened during the same time that President George W.
Bush nominated one of the former church members to the Supreme

Court. The media picked up on the split, immediately linked it to the nominee, and the incident was all over the news. As a result, even more people left the church.

The preaching pastor stepped into the role of senior pastor. In 2009, that senior pastor left for another church. When I came to candidate at the church, there were only 440 people still attending. Not many people, but lots of brokenness, mistrust, hurt, pain, and bitterness haunted the church hallways.

A Christ-Led Church

When you go into a new church, good preaching is paramount. Most people will say that life groups, family ministry, and worship are *the* most important things. Well, those things are important, but according to Thom Rainer and Ed Stetzer, the number one reason why people choose a church is the pastor and the preaching. I had to embrace this at the beginning of my tenure.

I accepted the position of senior pastor in January, 2010, and we moved to Dallas in the middle of February. I had been confirmed by a unanimous vote of the elders and 100% "yes" vote by the congregation. My first task was to create a preaching calendar. I decided that I would always plan out a year in advance every sermon I would preach (series, topic, Scripture, etc.) I also worked to be 3-4 weeks ahead in my sermon planning—and have kept that pace. Therefore, if I have a busy week, I know that I'm already four weeks ahead and can handle a busy week, without robbing my wife and kids of their time.

The beginning of every year would focus on Jesus. I initially wanted my first sermon series to be on Nehemiah and rebuilding the walls—Nehemiah is a great book for casting vision. However, after a conversation with a friend, I put aside what I thought was best since not everyone would be on the same page with me. I did know that everyone who was there loved Jesus—if I preached about Him, we'd all be on the same page. A longer sermon series on Jesus also gave me a chance to allow the congregation to get to know me, without challenging them right off the bat. Looking back on it, this was a wise move. Preaching on Jesus before any other sermon series built trust between the people and myself and allowed them to see my heart for Christ. As a result, I now preach a sermon series on Jesus every year.

The next thing I did was focus on expository preaching. Let me restate that: *applicable* expository preaching. I say "applicable" because a lot of expository preaching is dry and people would be better off reading a commentary. I don't believe preaching is truly expository unless it takes people through a passage *and* shows them the application for a 21st century world.

Some pastors have the perfect outline, the right word studies, and so on—if they were still a student in seminary, they'd be preaching a "senior sermon" in chapel. What I quickly learned is that the people wanted someone to not just *teach* the text but *live* the text—model the text, be transparent with the text, and exegete the relevance of the text for today.

Relationships First

To make changes in a church, a good friend told me that I needed "deposits in the bank." That person was right. I've had many friends from Bible college and seminary that have gone into churches and tried to make changes without having the trust of the elders, much less the congregation. Many young guys will go into traditional churches wearing jeans, change the worship style in the first month and cast a new vision without having the trust or respect of the people. This has proven to be a fatal mistake.

Learning from my friends' mistakes, I spent the first ninety days just investing in people. I didn't change a thing. I met with people, took people to meals, had people over to our home, built relationships with the elders, and grew in that way! After ninety days, I had some change in the bank. I spent it by reorganizing a couple of staff positions and moving a *big* communion table from the front of the auditorium. Believe it or not, moving the communion table was a *big* deal. Two of the most beloved elders in the church built that table. When it was moved, there was a hush over the crowd the first Sunday. The elder who got up to deliver the communion meditation cried through most of his talk because the table was gone. However, no one left as a result of the table. When people did gripe, they were met by individuals that had become acquainted with me and were assured of my heart for Christ.

After a few changes, I spent more time with people. I always made sure that a time of stability followed any change that was made. As a result, people were not worn down by change after change. I also always had the "deposits" in my bank growing. When big changes needed to happen, we were able to deal with it—all the while having the support of the elders and the church.

New Understanding of Eldership and Senior Pastor

When the senior pastor and executive staff are unwilling to lead, the church's board will easily fall into micromanaging the organization. After the split occurred, leadership was fractured in the church. As a result, the elders oversaw much of the daily operations of the church.

The elders hired an executive pastor to oversee the staff and a business administrator to oversee the finances. The executive pastor began reporting to the elder board, along with the senior pastor. When that began, there was an internal struggle between the staff; this encouraged the elders, all the more, to micromanage the situation.

An issue that was happening simultaneously was that the Spanish pastor was not getting leadership from the senior pastor or other staff members. Therefore, he set up his own "eldership" in the Spanish-speaking worship service. While I don't think that he did this with any malice, it still became a problem. The Spanish service wasn't teaching the same small group curriculum, had a different preaching calendar and different leadership. All of these issues, and more, needed to be resolved.

When I came to the church, the board agreed that they wanted to move towards being a "Christ-led, elder-protected, staff-directed" church. This means that the elders do the shepherding, cast vision with the senior pastor, and guard the church (doctrine, mission, vision, and values).

The staff runs the daily operations of the church and the only employee on the board is the senior pastor. I was able to hire and fire staff when I needed to and was able to delegate authority to anyone on staff as I saw necessary (I eventually hired an executive pastor). It is vital that if there is a change in the philosophy of the eldership, that the whole staff should know about it. By doing this, you will save a lot of heartache.

This concept is important: The larger your church gets, the harder it becomes for the board to direct the daily affairs of the staff. I'm convinced that some churches don't grow because their boards don't build a culture of trust and don't allow the staff to do what they were hired to do.

Now I understand that some churches will only get to be so big, possibly because of location, leadership of the pastor, or even the fact that, in God's sovereignty, He wants them to be only so big.

Below is a chart that I amended from Gary McIntosh's book, *One Size Doesn't Fit All* and Kent E. Fillinger's article, *The Church Size Matrix—Part 1*. It shows how most churches govern themselves, based on size:

Church Size	Attendance	Pastor Role	Decisions	Staff	Church Type
Small Church	35-249	Shepherd	Elders and Key Families	Solo pastor	Traditional
Medium Church	250-499	Administrator	Elders and Committees	A couple of specialists	Turn-around
Large Church	500-999	Leader	Elders and Staff	Multiple specialists	Transitional
Emerging Megachurch	1,000-1,999	Teacher/ Leader	Elders--BIG and Staff most	Teams of specialists	Transforming
Megachurch	2,000-9,999	Teacher/ Leader/ Visionary	Elders--BIG and Senior Staff	Division Leaders, many layers	Creative
Gigachurch	10,000+	Teacher/ Leader/ Visionary	Elders--BIG and Executive Staff Team	Division Leaders, many layers	Innovative

The danger that you have to face in such a model of elder-protected and staff-led churches is the elders becoming rubber stamps. Our elders are never seen as rubber stamps. Allowing the staff to lead in such a way allows them to focus on what they are biblically supposed to focus on. To accomplish this, we drafted an elder board policy manual, about twenty pages long, outlining the requirements of eldership, boardroom behavior, interaction with the senior pastor and staff, etc. This manual serves to protect the board, staff, and church from men who may desire the position of elder for the wrong reasons.

There were some elders that didn't agree with this philosophy. When I came to VVCC, we had eighteen elders and now we have twelve—and most of them are new. Unfortunately, some elders left because of disagreement with the new philosophy. Our church was blessed to have men that saw the role of unity in the church as more important than disputable matters on how to run an elder board. Some of the former elders are still at our church to this day. Even though they don't agree with the philosophy of eldership, they support the board in every decision and serve as great examples to the congregation. We are blessed to have such godly men at the church.

The Building of Momentum

God uses momentum to move a church forward. You have to have momentum to make the necessary changes that will glorify God through the church. Momentum can come through various avenues. For example, if you are a new pastor, your coming creates momentum. If you have growth, that creates momentum. A campaign or church-wide effort can create momentum. All of these things create momentum. The hard part is sustaining that momentum. How in the world can one do that?

Momentum can be sustained by having a visionary mindset. In other words, always be thinking ahead of everyone else. Seek the Lord on what He would have you do next. As a senior pastor, I need to be thinking ahead with the elders.

For example, people are encouraged with the hiring of a new associate pastor. A huge church outreach a couple of months later creates new momentum. The key is to plan out your 1-year, 5-year, and 10-year plan so that you have momentum builders.

So far, we have been able to ride the waves of intentional momentum-building events. In just a couple of weeks, we will unveil our new elementary-age worship venue. This will be huge for our church!

On another note, planning ahead creates goals. Too many pastors operate without any kind of goal or idea of where God has called their church to go. A lack of goals shows no direction. No direction is a momentum killer!

New Worship Service

By the time I got to the church, VVCC had dropped from three worship services to one worship service in a 1,500-seat auditorium. The service was usually 90-100 minutes long, and had ten minutes of announcements, worship that was a conglomeration of hymns and 90's praise music, and long communion meditations. At one time they had excellent traditional music and great musical productions. After the split, that had fallen by the wayside.

Changing the worship service was key to pointing the church in a new direction. We began by updating their version of contemporary music. While they were still singing late 1990's worship music, much had been written since then.

Our church elders have a goal of embracing an identity as a multigenerational church, so we still sing hymns. Now these hymns can be sung in a Chris Tomlin way, a David Crowder way, a Hillsong way—or even in the traditional way—but we always do two hymns.

I had underestimated just how toxic the response would be to the new worship music style. I still have a file of e-mails—critical notes from people regarding the worship style, stage design, and dress of the band. It's amazing that the one thing that we are there to do (worship) can so easily divide churches. Some of the sweetest people you can hope to meet wrote me some of the worst e-mails. People that took us out to dinner when we moved to the church, filled our pantry, and brought us meals were now waging an unintended campaign against the worship style.

New Staff

One of the positive things about VVCC was that its building and land were paid for. A negative reaction to this victory was "overstaffing." The church was so overstaffed when I got there that people had no idea what to do. It was apparent that the church had too many staff members, many of them struggling in their positions. Some of them were in positions that had too much responsibility while others were in positions that underutilized their skills.

In my first three years at the church, I released fifteen people, reorganized several positions, and hired several new staff members. I would *not* recommend this unless you are sure that you have plenty of "deposits" in the bank, the support of the elders, and a green light from God.

Hiring an executive pastor to oversee the administration of the staff and finances was key since I'm not good at that. I've learned to focus on my strengths and delegate my weaknesses. Paperwork and details are not my strong suit. Delegating my weaknesses has been important in my being a good leader for our church.

Bringing in the right staff and forming an elite team have been crucial. Without these people, we would not be where we are today. Here's what I've learned about staffing issues:

1. Hire slowly
2. Fire quicker than you think you should
3. Be overly generous when you fire
4. Hire specialists
5. Hire people you trust, even if you're accused of hiring your friends
6. Form a human resources team to help with details since this is becoming a bigger issue in the church
7. When you hire, look for three main things besides doctrine: Character, Competency and Chemistry.

External Focus vs. Internal Focus

When an animal is hurt, it will go into the corner and lick its wounds. That's exactly what was happening at Valley View Christian Church when I first arrived. The people were still hurting from the split. Instead of reaching where God had sovereignly put them, they were focusing on tons of Bible study. There were Sunday school classes that were not designed to do outreach. No real-life groups were taking place. No outreach to the community or the Dallas/Fort Worth metroplex. Nothing was happening.

I started preaching a sermon series called "Contagious Faith" where we discussed how we, as a church, could do better outreach to the community, city and world. This was amazing! From this study we started two ministries: Blessing Teen Parents (ministering to teen parents in high schools) and Serving Our Students (a daily after-school outreach to a lower-income apartment building). This spread to our Sunday schools doing their own outreaches. Today, we have a Halloween festival and a Christmas outreach … and our people are thinking of how they can do more!

As a result, our church has become more multiethnic. One of our goals was to be a multiethnic church. We desired to become a Revelation 7 church—a church of every tongue, tribe, and nation before the throne of the Lamb. Our church was physically located in the middle of a multiethnic community, but Walmart was more multiethnic than our church. Through VVCC's intentionality of outreach, we showed the community that we cared. Our church grew and we started to look more like heaven on earth!

Family Life Ministry

In Valley View Christian Church's "popular" days, they focused on everything that happened on stage. They had orchestras, concerts, huge organ music, and great choir robes. What they never had was a focus on the family. As the demographics around the community changed, the church itself never changed. When I arrived at the church, we did a demographic study of the surrounding area. Over 55% of the surrounding area was between the ages of 20-39. Another 20% were 0-19 years of age. So, 75% of the surrounding demographics were young—and the church was not.

We responded by spending the majority of our staff hires on retooling the Family Life Department and improving the Family Life facilities. As a result, one of our biggest areas of growth has been the Family Life area. We've seen many young families come, staying because their children were being cared for and discipled.

Results

1. People come, people go.
My biggest fear through this period was losing people. When I say that, I mean losing church members. The fact is that when you're in a turnaround church, you'll lose the people you want if you do nothing, and you'll lose the people you need to lose if you do something. I know that sounds harsh, but it's true. We had 440 on my first Sunday. Three years later we are running around 1,000 in attendance. To date, we've had about 200 or more people leave our church. If some were to leave today, experience shows that it never feels good. I keep focusing on the new people and the changed lives that are there—and focus on the people that aren't there yet, but are coming in the future.

2. Staff is shining.
We have a healthier staff culture where people feel safe and secure. Staff members are working hard and developing new leaders. There is a chemistry between the staff and elders like never before.

3. Worship is stellar.
I dare to say that we have the best worship service format that we've ever had. The care and attention that we are putting into this is *huge*. People coming to the church are influenced by the preaching and the excellence of worship.

4. Outreach is abounding.
More of our people are taking hold of the expectation that they are to serve and share. Ministries have been started like outreaches to teen moms, after school programs, etc.

5. Vision is flowing.
We try to be a church that casts vision all the time—from the sermon to small groups to staff meetings. The vision of where God is taking our church is being celebrated and promoted.

6. Risks are being taken.

One of the most important things that a leader must do is to take risks. The larger and healthier churches understand that risk-taking is vital to the growth and success of the church.

Final Thoughts

It is truly exhilarating to see what God has brought us through in the major turnaround at Valley View over the past couple of years. While we are certainly not there yet, it is exciting to trust God for the future. We still need to work on areas in our ministry, such as reorganizing and rethinking how we "do missions," the cultivation of small groups and Bible fellowships. We also hope to invest more money into ministry and retool our facilities for more effective ministry. These are some of the challenges and opportunities that lie ahead.

THE TRUST FACTOR
Creating a Culture of Trust That Thrives in a Climate of Crisis
D. Scott Barfoot

The other day we had a meeting in my office with a team of leaders at the seminary. In my work space sits a square table with four aging chairs surrounding it. While these wooden chairs are a little worn, the cushioned fabric makes them comfortable.

However, there is one chair where the glue is no longer holding its frame tightly together. So when one of the participants showed up and sat in this chair, he felt it sway. It startled him, and he quickly moved to a different chair.

"Scott, you need to have facilities come over and fix this chair," he said.

I agreed.

Another participant entered my office and sat down in that same chair. He too felt it shift sideways. Then he moved to a different seat.

There was something unsettling about the sway of the chair that made it difficult to trust.

I've had this recurring conversation over the years with different people, in different parts of the country, around different church contexts. You've likely heard the general script which goes something like this:

They say, "We've decided to leave the church."

We say, "Oh, really? Is everything okay?"

They say, "Yes, everything is okay. There is just …" They hesitate. "There is just something that doesn't seem right for us now. So we've decided to leave."

This type of speak—while not always the case—often translates to, "I don't trust the church anymore." And they move on.

Some time ago, I was chatting with a pastor who had invested much of himself in a couple of key families at his growing church. When these families communicated their plans to leave, it completely broadsided him. I empathized with the pastor because I have been in his shoes. At some point along the way, something happens to people's trust and they will move on as a result.

In today's church organizations, visible flaws and failures among clergy have caused an undercurrent of distrust towards pastors. Lay persons are often cynical and even suspicious of pastoral leaders. Not only does this make it challenging for the pastor to cultivate trust, but it makes it nearly impossible for him to lead effectively.

Often, due in part to a breakdown of trust, a growing number of pastors experience a forced exit from their post. This is no surprise, given what Thom Rainer observes in *Surprising Insights from the Unchurched*. He states that the average pastor's tenure lasts less than four years at any one ministry post. How can a church organization advance with such frequent changes in leadership?

As a result of the disintegration of interpersonal trust between the clergy and lay persons, significant setbacks to emotional/organizational health, growth and ministry effectiveness are experienced by individual pastors, lay persons and church organizations.

I am convinced that every church leader *must* more intentionally consider the pressing issue of trust before it is too late. This is especially true in the high crisis environment in which we all too often find ourselves.

Trust can make or break a leader, a team, or a ministry. Trust is that central factor that aligns, synchronizes and oils the gears of unified diversity. Trust propels an organization forward to reach its mission and change the world. As Les Csorba says in his book, entitled *Trust*: "Trust is the essence of leadership."

It is every pastor's responsibility to help *create a culture of trust that can thrive in a climate of crisis*. Now is the time, as you read this chapter, to consider these vital questions:

- Am I confident in God's shepherding in my life

and leadership?

- Do I trust those on my leadership team and do they trust me?
- Do we have positive trust-building dynamics in our organization?
- Could our current trust levels withstand the turbulent forces of a major crisis?
- How am I creating a culture of trust that can thrive in a climate of crisis?

Together, in the next few pages, we will explore these important questions. However, by God's grace, only you and those that work closest with you will be able to contextualize the core concepts outlined here into the life stream of your leadership and ministry.

1) Forge your personal trust core.

One evening, my wife Debbie and I stayed up until the early hours of the morning in deep conversation. We talked about our relationship and the challenges of pastoral ministry before us. I told her that whatever we encounter in life and ministry—the good, the bad, the ugly—no matter what happens, that she should keep her trust in the Lord Jesus and not in me. She agreed and asked that I, too, should keep my trust in the Lord and not in her.

This mutual commitment to place our ultimate confidence in the Lord became a part of forging *our personal trust core*. This trust core, however, was tested through several years of major personal and ministry crises while serving in the Washington, DC area.

As the saying goes, the hits kept on coming:

- The founding pastor transitioned to a new ministry which quickly thrust me into a lead role (more about that later).
- We struggled for six years with infertility and finally conceived. A few weeks after conception Debbie became unusually sick with pregnancy-induced hyperemesis gravidarum (very extreme morning sickness). She couldn't keep food or liquids down, and was continuously malnourished

and dehydrated—bedridden for more than half of her pregnancy.

- The labor and delivery turned into a nightmare scenario when she developed preeclampsia. The baby had severe oxygen deprivation which led to an emergency C-section and a terribly long recovery for Debbie.

- Our precious Davey couldn't open his eyelids more than 1mm—at three months he had his first of several surgical procedures to address his condition. Many years later, we discovered that some of the pregnancy and birth issues contributed to his low vision and shut-down sections of his brain.

- Just prior to Davey's birth, 9/11 happened. One of our church members was at the Pentagon during the 2001 attack. We thanked God for His protection over her, a single mom. Many others in the church family were directly impacted by this historic event.

- There were deadly sniper attacks, where six people were killed, in our Maryland neighborhood.

- We moved from Maryland to northern Virginia to be closer to the church at around the same time as our son's birth, adding more stress.

- The church went through some major relocation transitions. One involved a forty-day termination of a lease agreement, we had to move from a permanent worship facility to a local hotel and then to a school with a mobile church set-up.

- Other conflictual situations were at times emotionally consuming for me as a young pastor, trying to lead in the midst of much personal and organizational crisis.

I am so grateful for Debbie. We weathered this storm and several others. We continue—after sixteen years of marriage and ministry together—to love, respect and encourage each other while finding our ultimate hope and trust in the Lord Jesus Christ.

Forging our personal trust core is the first step in creating a culture of trust that can thrive in a climate of crisis.

We can do this in a couple of ways: First, by recognizing our own brokenness and the brokenness of those who work with us. Second, by anchoring ourselves in Jesus as our Good Shepherd, the only One who is worthy of our ultimate allegiance and trust.

Brokenness

This personal trust core first acknowledges the biblical truth that all people are broken from sin (Rom. 3:23). Every ministry leader who has trusted in Jesus has a positional standing of righteousness before God. However, every leader this side of heaven continues to have idiosyncrasies, limitations, personal flaws and blind spots. Even seasoned pastoral leaders who know Christ and are growing in Him must contend with the sinful nature, the attacks of Satan, and the lure of the world. The Christian life is a spiritual warfare (Eph. 6:10) and not a casual stroll in the park.

This genuine conviction of our own brokenness and struggle with our depravity must drive us to our knees in prayer, in utter and total dependence on the Lord (Neh. 1:1-10). It compels us to give other maturing believers permission to speak into our lives (Gal. 6:2). Recognition of this reality should cause us to welcome Christ-centered, loving accountability.

It is important to remind those you lead that you are human. Hero worship in evangelical circles seems commonplace today. Please don't get me wrong. Honor needs to be given where honor is due. There is a place for public recognition and personal affirmation. But even the greatest leaders are human.

This is what I found so powerful at Prof. Howard Hendricks' recent memorial service. Here was a man with an unbelievable legacy of Christian leadership. Yet, during the service, his family and friends gave a high-definition picture of not only his accomplishments, but also his humanity and dependence on his Savior, Jesus Christ. As his student in the 90's, and during his teaching in the Doctor of Ministry program, I never realized how much he had struggled with depression over the years.

There is a false belief that we have to be perfect or present ourselves as perfect. Some of us might believe we are closer to perfection than anyone else. On the other hand, some of us think that we are so inadequate that we question how God could use us. These extremes are both dangerous and far from the truth.

It reminds me of what my late grandfather would say, "Remember you are no better than anyone else, but you're no worse than anyone else either." This is the biblical concept of thinking soberly about oneself (Rom. 12:3). Popular author and speaker John Maxwell was right when he noted that people see us either better than we really are or worse than we really are. God sees us for who we really are and for what He wants us to become. Unfortunately, the church ministry cultures we create can inadvertently feed into a perfect-pastor-on-a-pedestal ethos. People start seeing us better than we really are, only to become disillusioned when the reality of our human imperfections surface.

I experienced this struggle in my own pastoral ministry. As a young pastor, I feared failing to meet the expectations of the congregation. One weekend I was sick with the flu. Late Saturday evening, I decided I would show a video of a sermon—preached by a well-known pastor—instead of trying to preach the following morning. This was the first and only time I did this at the church over a five-year period of a regular preaching ministry.

After the service, a couple of individuals were upset. They questioned why I had showed a video in the service rather than preaching myself. Even though I had been ill, they were not pleased with the decision to play a videoed sermon. Of course there were other issues going on that brought another layer of complexity to this issue. Physically I felt terrible, but I also struggled with feelings of guilt and failure as a pastor. When I called up a close friend who was also in pastoral ministry, he prayed with me and encouraged me to ignore the criticism, stating that it was good for the congregation to see that I was human.

It is okay to be a leader and be human because our trust is in God and not ourselves. We are all so frail. Our ultimate confidence cannot be in ourselves or another leader—even ones we rightfully admire and respect. Our confidence must be in God alone.

Our personal trust core shifts our confidence from ourselves and our performance to Him who is worthy of our total trust. It is the biblical mindset that God is good. He has my best interests at heart, as one small but significant part in His grand and glorious plan. It is the anchored confidence that I can trust Him, regardless of the winds and waves of my circumstances, knowing that all things work together for the good in accordance with His purposes (Rom. 8:28). This unwavering, resilient trust in God is at the crux of forging a personal trust core.

If there is any threat to our personal trust core, it is when our hearts become hardened by disappointment, hurt or failure. That is when we are tempted to replace trust in God with a cemented, self-protective, self-trust.

Our Good Shepherd

Knowing the Lord Jesus as our Good Shepherd helps keep our hearts soft and moldable, like fresh potter's clay. It encourages us in our relationship with God, self and others to rise above any kind of disappointment that may come our way.

Some time ago, I relived an unforgettable childhood memory while reflecting on Phillip Keller's book, *A Shepherd Looks at Psalm 23*. Keller describes, "shall not want" as being completely satisfied with the Lord's management of my life.

One wintry night, my grandfather and I started chores in the snow-covered, six-generation barn in Owen Sound, Ontario, Canada. My duty that evening was to give the sheep their portion of grain. I filled a large bucket from a nearby granary and carried it back to the sheep pen. After maneuvering through the crowded maze of bleating sheep, I poured the grain into their feeding trough for all to enjoy.

Suddenly, as I stepped out of the pen, a selfish ewe charged her way through the flock toward the feeding trough. Butting the other ewes aside, she began to gulp down the grain greedily. Then, just seconds after this aggressive behavior, she abruptly stopped eating, jerked back from the feeder, and began gasping for air.

With great urgency, my grandfather told me to climb back into the pen to help her clear her throat. I quickly made my way to the desperate sheep and tried to open up her airway with my fingers. My efforts were in vain. Moments later, we stood staring at the lifeless ewe on the ground before us.

I will never forget my grandfather's words that pierced the silence. "You foolish sheep!" My grandfather had consistently and unfailingly provided the daily portion of grain for her benefit and well-being. Why then did the ewe forget her good shepherd's loving care?

Am I fully and completely satisfied with my Good Shepherd's loving leadership and management of my life?

It is a trust issue, isn't it? If we are not walking in step with the Spirit in a trusting relationship—trusting Him who is perfect in every way—how in the world can we build trust among our leadership team and congregation, people who, like us, are flawed, imperfect and limited in every way?

Let's face reality: we sheep are messy. Only the Good Shepherd can clean us up and lead us forward on a path of righteousness.

As we wrap our minds around the truth that God is our Good Shepherd and that He cares for us as His workmanship, with divine meaning and purpose, we can forge our personal trust core and take that first step in cultivating a healthy framework for trust.

I mentioned earlier about our first post-seminary church where the founding pastor transitioned to a new ministry. In March 1999, we headed to Washington, DC where I took the role of assistant pastor at a growing, multiethnic church. This church plant was made up of predominately Asian Americans, many of whom were young professionals serving in a variety of roles—with noteworthy levels of local and international influence. Within four months of my arrival, the founding pastor asked me to step into a lead role because of a pressing family health emergency. I didn't realize it at the time but my mission would be to lead the transition from the founding pastor to the founding vision over a period of five years.

We all loved the founding pastor and were deeply saddened by his unexpected departure. Ministry was now filled with a new level of challenge for me. Here I was, a Caucasian, twenty-something, Canadian farm boy, now called to lead an Asian American church full of young professionals in the hustle and bustle of Washington, DC. "Lord, how in the world can I lead this church?" I thought to myself.

I still remember the uncertainty and anxiety in my heart—and among many of the church members. Some questioned whether the young church could survive this kind of major leadership transition. As I began to feel the weight of my new role, I was completely overwhelmed by the task. I felt like Frodo in the *Lord of the Rings* as he wrestled with being the chosen one to carry the ring. However, God reassured me that He was in complete control of the situation.

There was one particular day, just weeks before the founding pastor was about to complete his service at the church. Several of us were at the church office when we received a thank you card in the mail. The card was from a technology firm in the area and their kind note said something like this,

"We want to thank you and your church for your ministry in the community. Some of your members have been the glue that have held our company together through some very difficult times and we wanted to say thank you."

As we read the card together, encouragement in God's work in and through the church filled our hearts. But then something shocking happened that literally knocked us to our knees in speechless thanksgiving.

At the back of the card was a check. It was a cash gift of $100,000.

Now I know God doesn't always work that way. But at that moment in time, it was a powerful reminder that God was in control. He was with us. In the midst of the rapids of this unanticipated transition, He would see us through. And He did see us through this most challenging and fruitful season of ministry.

We can't place ultimate trust in ourselves, other people or our circumstances. Only the Lord, as our Good Shepherd, can anchor our souls in dependent confidence. My personal trust core is that central cohesive force that provides emotional and spiritual stability to trust the Lord in total dependence. It unleashes us to take risks, believing God to work through the situation. It lifts us above the otherwise straightjacketing circumstances we might face.

Forging our own personal trust core is the first pivotal step in creating a culture of trust that can thrive in a climate of crisis. But there is another important step for us to consider.

2) Establish a relationship of trust with your core team.

The second step in creating a culture of trust that can thrive in a climate of crisis requires us to *establish relationships of trust with our core team*.

It is never too soon to intentionally and thoughtfully strengthen relationships of trust within our leadership team. Before we unpack this further, I am defining relational trust as a responsible act of faith where one person believes in and voluntarily depends on another in the context of service.

Contemporary researchers have discovered common antecedents of interpersonal trust. I am grateful to scholars/ practitioners such as Bruce Avolio, Bernard Bass, Warren Bennis, John Butler, James Davis, Kurt Dirks, James Kouzes, Roger Mayer, Burt Nanus, Barry Posner, John Reed, David Schoorman, Bruce Winston, and many others who, over the past several years, have contributed to my thinking and leadership practice on establishing interpersonal trust.

While these common trust-building characteristics differ throughout literature, researchers have arrived at similar conclusions regarding factors influencing the formation of trust. I would suggest that there are four primary trust building characteristics that every ministry leader can assimilate, in the grace and power of God, to promote relationships of trust.

Personal qualities such as *integrity, skill, communication* and *presence* are four potent, trust-building traits that we can embody over time to help create and sustain a culture of trust with our core team.

Integrity: Walk the talk

Trust-building leadership is about integrity of the heart. There is nothing that ignites relationships of trust more powerfully than a pastoral leader who consistently "walks the talk," exemplifying congruency, consistency and fairness.

When there is a *congruency between a leader's words and actions, and the organization's guiding principles*, a leader is known as a person of integrity. Leaders must be who they are wherever they go, with a maturing conformity to the character of Christ—in alignment with the mission, core values and beliefs of the organization.

Integrity also includes the leaders *consistency*. Do I do what I say I am going to do? Am I following through on commitments made? These are important measures of a leader's consistency. Over the years I have found refreshment in listening to the late Fred Smith, Sr. speak on Christian leadership. Leader consistency is one area he underscored.

"We can't be a leader and an emotional yo-yo. The consistency of a leader is very important." Mr. Smith expressed this in a recorded message archived at breakfastwithfred.com.

I vividly recall Fred telling the story of how he inherited his mentor's Bible. He highlighted that this man's Bible was marked with all sorts of notes. But they were not just written there to *teach* but to *live by*. Fred's mentor modeled integrity and it strengthened Fred's relationship of trust with him.

Fairness or justice is an often forgotten aspect of integrity that accentuates the fair treatment of persons within the organization. Establishing clear and consistent policies and procedures for church business, decision-making, hiring/firing staff, church discipline, and conflict resolution can enhance trust.

Contemporary researchers have found an association between procedural justice and organizational trust. More specifically, it has been observed that fairness in the treatment of an individual is a vital predictor of interpersonal trust among employees and senior management. There is evidence that a fair work climate promotes safety and openness that increases interpersonal trust among members in the organization.

Skill: Swing to meet the ball

If integrity is a matter of the heart, skill is that matter of the hands. Psalm 78:72 says, "And David shepherded them with integrity of heart; with skillful hands he led them."

Skill is used interchangeably with ability in the trust literature and can be defined as the *technical and interpersonal competencies of a leader within a particular sphere of service*. My friend and mentor, John Reed, would say it like this, "Just keep swinging to meet the ball."

Pastoral leaders must always keep swinging to meet the ball in the playing field of ministry. In the process, each swing refines their technical skills in areas such as leadership, preaching, counseling, administration, and interpersonal relations. The latter may be more difficult for some.

David Schuller, at the June 1985 Association of Theological School's Conference on Student Development in Theological Education, observed the pressing issue of interpersonal incompetence among ministry leaders. He outlined nine harmful patterns that can give rise to interpersonal incompetence. I believe these are timeless, relevant concerns for us to consider as we pursue interpersonal competence to promote trust.

1) An inability to listen and see the whole picture of a particular situation, resulting in the offering of inappropriate advice.
2) A pattern of blaming others rather than accepting personal responsibility.
3) Negligence in either over-delegating or under-delegating responsibility.
4) Relationally incapable of forming common loyalties with others.
5) An inability to maintain congruency in their words and behaviors or follow-through with promises.
6) Holding onto an insatiable need for approval from everyone, all of the time, in order to find emotional support.
7) A view of reality that is colored by one's own internal struggles.
8) Easily intimidated by those who do not think the same way.
9) Not able to listen and support others on an emotional level while intellectually disagreeing with them.

The technical and relational competence of a leader is considered to be a strong predictor of interpersonal trust. It is also found that leaders are more likely to trust in a co-worker or subordinate based on his or her performance.

As leaders set their own lifelong learning outcomes to grow in Christ-likeness, knowledge and skills, there is a level of core competence attained to fulfill the task at hand with excellence, efficiency and fruitfulness. A growing leader, therefore, is a trust-building leader. Followers are more likely to have confidence in that leader as one who is capable of meeting and exceeding his or her leadership responsibilities.

Am I intentionally learning new skills in order to grow in the knowledge and grace of the Lord Jesus Christ and improve my serve?

Communication: Talk the walk

There is another crucial attribute that complements both integrity and skill in building relationships of trust among a leader's core team. It is the quintessential trust-building trait of mission-focused, relevant, and sincere leader communication.

Leader communication is the *process of conveying vital inspiration and information to promote applied biblical truth for spiritual and organizational transformation.* These leaders inform, inspire and link others through their public preaching, group sharing, individual conversations, and written communications. They provide clarity, meaning, resources and hope for others, to help accomplish the mission before them through their communications.

Ministry leaders develop their mastery of "talking the walk" through biblically-based storytelling, clearly translating the mission, vision, values and beliefs of the organization into the everyday language of the people they lead. Further, these leaders kindle critical thinking in the minds of others by spurring them to approach challenges with imagination and innovation. Ultimately, these leaders paint a compelling picture of a preferred future state which excites others, inducing them to personally add value and contribute to the organization in reaching its destination.

Today's technological world opens several new channels for effective, trust-enhancing communication. For example, social media such as Facebook, Google+, LinkedIn, Twitter, and Wordpress can be a positive way to engage in regular church-wide communication and dialogue, beyond the routine weekly services. While grapevine-like in nature, it is much more powerful and can be strategically utilized to enhance openness and trust within an organization.

Am I regularly communicating the mission and heartbeat of our organization in ways that connect to the mind, emotions and volition of my core team?

Presence: Be there for others

Personal presence is the fourth leg to the stool of trust. Like integrity, skill and communication, personal presence is absolutely indispensable in trust-building relationships. Presence is *the manifestation of a leader's genuine care, compassion, and benevolence toward another.* Ministry leaders can build trust by radiating a Barnabas-like pastoral presence through receptivity, encouragement, and prayer with team members.

First, *receptivity* is an important ingredient in personal presence. A receptive leader is one who makes himself or herself available and diligently employs active, empathetic listening, seeking to understand what followers say. In addition, it is being open and responsive to new ideas, feedback and even criticism with a non-defensive spirit. Receptive leaders are able to value and respond to feedback in an objective, gracious manner.

Second, personal presence incorporates supportive *encouragement* to others. Ministry leaders see and bring out the best in others through insightful observations and/or questions, affirmation and reflective discussion. Encouragement can help others reframe basic assumptions, refine limited thinking, renew a broken spirit, and release a new idea.

Third, *prayer* centers both receptivity and encouragement in an ultimate trust and dependence on the Lord. It recognizes the great potential for healthy relationships of trust to be formed in the grace and power of a great and ever-present God.

These expressions of loyalty and goodwill in personal presence can enhance trust among a pastoral leader's core team. Am I available and intentional in offering receptive support, encouragement and prayer?

Summary

It is every pastor's greatest challenge and opportunity to help create a culture of trust that can thrive in a climate of crisis. The first step requires us as leaders to *forge our own personal trust core* by recognizing the reality of our own brokenness, anchoring ourselves in Jesus as our Good Shepherd. He alone is worthy of our ultimate allegiance and trust.

The second step in creating a culture of trust that can thrive in a climate of crisis requires us, as leaders, to reach out and *establish relationships of trust with our core team* as an overflow of our personal trust core. As we embody the characteristics of *integrity*—the congruency between my words and actions, and my organization's guiding principles; *skill*—the technical and interpersonal competencies I possess within my particular sphere of service; *communication*—the process where I convey vital inspiration and information to cultivate applied biblical truth for spiritual and organizational transformation; and *presence*—the manifestation of genuine care, compassion, and benevolence toward members of the team, we can further establish and enhance relationships of trust which will permeate our core leader and church community. This will lay a foundation and framework for greater ministry effectiveness in reaching the new horizons God has for us while serving our ministry organizations.

A CRISIS OF POSITIVE PROPORTIONS
$225,000 Unused

David R. Fletcher

It was a dreary night in February when Tami and I had dinner with the couple who had put up $225,000 for a future ministry. Though it would have been easier to avoid the subject, I had to raise it. "It looks like God is taking us to California, so what does that mean about your donation to our Asian work?"

This last story in our examination of "crisis leadership" is about turning down almost a quarter of a million dollars. God provided a large deal of money through some gracious donors in Dallas, and, for the first time in my life, I was leaving "money on the table."

What? Turning down money? Not using God's provision? How could anyone leave that much money on the table? Such is the tale of my "folly of following God." It is a leadership crisis of positive proportions.

A Crisis of Terrible Proportions

In most situations, a crisis is a terrible thing. It is a challenge that we must live up to. It is an intrusion into our physical or mental well-being; an emergency surgery, a family member in a car crash, a tornado heading for your town. In short, we consider a crisis to be a bummer, a bad day or a terrible season of life. And so it is, most of the time.

I have long maintained that seminary well prepared me for many a crisis in the church. However, it did not prepare me to deal with success. The terms *crisis* and *success* appear to be antithetical. There are so many hard bumps in life that we are better equipped to handle a crisis than we are to handle success.

Tami and I have had our set of challenges. If I were to write about our house in Austin that wouldn't sell and how we paid seven months of mortgage on an empty house—that would be a crisis story. The crisis abated—not by selling the house but by renting it. I said *abated* because now we have issues of being landlords. Just this month the clothes dryer went out, so we had to replace the washer and dryer. At the same time, the pool developed a leak … the upstairs bathroom leaked water into the garage … let's add in the refrigerator that needed repairing … and then the air conditioner needed work. All of this happened within four weeks.

Those are the types of crises that easily resonate with us. It seems that all of us are well prepared in the "school of hard knocks" to receive such events. There is that wonderful expression, "waiting for the other shoe to drop." We just know that one bit of bad news might be followed by another. I'm going to collectively call all of these events in our lives, *A Crisis of Terrible Proportions*.

A Crisis of Positive Proportions

How do we handle success? What do you do when God gives so many options that one must choose between some equally good things? How do we handle too much "blessing" by God?

For most of us, there are two ways that we determine God's favor and support of what option we should choose:

- Did He provide the money for it?
- Are our friends, family and advisors in support of it?

I would wager a guess (and that word "wager" is used judiciously here) that most of us see that the provision of money is the easiest way to determine God's will.

Unfortunately, so many of us are such raging capitalists that we think that money is what makes the world go around. We see money as the most important thing in life. While we try to not be materialists, most of us have as many "toys" as our neighbors. Materialism is the cultural waters where we all live. It is seemingly impossible to swim against the tide of materialism. We try to get to the safe shore of inner contentment but are often swept up in materialism's powerful current.

I would put forth that because of this tide of materialism that surges into every corner of our homes, our grid for making decisions is based largely on money. Before this essay gets too philosophical, let me give you the gist of our story.

Tami and I found that our church ministry in the Midwest was drawing to a close. The senior pastor that we dearly loved found that he was not a good fit with that church. I'm not "throwing him under the bus," as these were his public and recorded words as to why he was leaving. The church was a large one, with about 5,000 people in worship each week. We had experienced a wonderful time of ministry there and wondered what we should do next.

As we prayed and asked God about our next steps, we realized that perhaps we should explore expanding both a *consulting work* with churches in the U.S. and a *teaching work* overseas. This was quite a departure from the work of being an executive pastor, but, after some time thinking about it, it seemed like a good plan.

As we shared these thoughts with some dear friends, they saw the vision for expanding the work overseas. Along the way, they declared their intent to give $225,000, over a three-year period, to make this work possible.

And indeed, these friends began to make good on their promise. They donated $53,000 in 2012 toward that endeavor. All of us were delighted that some great overseas work was being planned.

The Crisis Unfolds

As though a confirmation of the plans and the money, an invitation soon arrived from two different people to expand the work into two countries in east Asia. If I were Gideon, the conclusion would have been that we should move forward. This seemed to be God's loud voice saying, "Yes, do it!"

Yet, God does not always speak in a mighty voice. Jesus calmed the waves on the Sea of Galilee with a great voice. In contrast, God spoke to Elijah in a quiet voice. There are many voices that God uses. Just because the storm is raging doesn't mean that God has to raise His voice. He might ... but He doesn't have to!

With the consulting work and international teaching work, it looked like my thirty-plus years in pastoral ministry were drawing to a close. My time of being an Executive Pastor seemed to be over. I had angst about this change of career, so I talked with a friend about this. Nathan had exited pastoral ministry to become a respected consultant. He affirmed that the cause of my angst was leaving one career position for another—and he told of how he had walked that path.

Many people thought that I should leave pastoral ministry and become a consultant and trainer. There was a good basis for it. While doing pastoral ministry, I had started the XPastor website. Over the years it had grown into a micro-niche site, giving free advice to thousands of church leaders each year. It received over 300,000 visits each year.

Tami and I had hosted an annual conference for church leaders, with a solid ten-year history. There had also been regional workshops and events. We judiciously used our vacation time from church to work with scores of hundreds of leaders around the country.

In addition to this, I had made a ten-year commitment to begin a Doctor of Ministry program in India. The goal of the program was to inaugurate it, run it and turn it over to a national. In the seventh year, we had our first "batch of graduates" (as they say in India) and appointed a wonderfully competent and gifted Indian to be the next director.

It was two of the students in that program who invited me to come to their countries and start similar programs. Sri Lanka and Myanmar seemed to be calling! The money was there and everything seemed right to move in that direction.

From a business perspective, there was every good reason to become a consultant and expand our teaching ministry overseas.

Yet, do we determine what we should do by our own common sense? Do we go by what seems to be right? Even as we pray, and our plans seem to be endorsed by God, is this what we should do?

There were so many positive elements to this story. From a materialistic perspective, everything shouted, "Do it! Be your own boss. Focus on just what you want to do! Move back to Austin. Travel to Asia three times a year. You are good at teaching and organizing major programs. Do it!"

Changes in the Plan

Yet, this was my time to discover in a new way that the wisdom of God is mere foolishness to men. And what a surprise and leadership crisis it was! It was a crisis of positive proportions.

One of the first things we discovered was that our partner in ministry needed a break. He had worked through an enormous personal loss and specifically asked for a break. His loving and young wife had fought a hard battle with cancer—and she lost the physical fight but won the spiritual reward of a new body with Christ. We had made many plans with him but his personal life needed a time of healing and rebuilding.

That was a wake-up call. Perhaps God was letting us taste all of these wonderful plans but was saying "not now" or perhaps "never." The challenge was that we were beginning to like the new plans that we sensed God had for us. However, we now had some mixed signals about them.

Then there was the e-mail from Jac, a long-time ministry colleague. He wanted to know if I would talk to a Senior Pastor about joining their staff as his Executive Pastor. While in India—and it seems that many of my life changes happen while I am in India—I read the e-mail. The request was from a church in Orange County, our home area. We had never thought about moving back to Orange County. In fact, we had a slight aversion to moving back to such a rich place as my hometown of Newport Beach. Their shopping center called Fashion Island was a beacon of flaunted wealth, clothes and cars. No, this was not the place for us to return to after an absence of 33 years.

Being in contact with many churches through the XPastor network, I get several such "talk to us" e-mails each year. My reply wanted to be a simple "no." Yet, being theologically trained, one cannot give a simple "no." Instead, one is taught by the good counsel of those trained in the Scriptures to say, "No, unless God works a miracle."

Why not say no? We had the promise of $225,000 and they had begun their gift with $53,000 already. We had put our house in Ohio on the market and it had a contract on it. We had a rental contract on an apartment in Austin for eighteen months; we would live there until the renters in our Austin house moved out. We had transferred our mail to an Austin post office box. We had offers of ministry in east Asia. Friends, counselors and family all said, "Move to Austin."

Positive Proportions

A crisis of positive proportions is many times in the little things. A crisis is not always about terrible things. It can be about trying to decide the best avenues to follow, instead of settling for the average or the good. It is about saying, "God you can do a miracle and it would take a miracle to change my course right now." God is active in the world and ready to change events when He chooses—not when we choose—and that is why we call His intervention "miraculous."

A few days after I had received the e-mail from Fullerton, another e-mail came. The contract on our Akron house had fallen through. The buyer's house did not appraise as they hoped and so they had to withdraw from buying our house. This was *not* yet a watershed moment. It was just an interesting issue.

Tami and I talked it through and decided that we should let go of the apartment in Austin. It seemed financially unwise to keep a rental apartment in Austin and have an unsold house in Akron. What if the Akron house took months or years to sell? We had experienced that before in selling a prior house. We could be in a terrible place financially. So, at a loss of close to a thousand dollars, we broke the contract with the apartment in Austin. We figured we could still do our consulting and overseas work from Akron, at least until the Akron house sold.

While it is challenging to share some of the details—and some will see it as travelogue—the core issues are in the real life and times that we lived. There wasn't a grand out-of-body experience here. We were dealing with huge and wonderful issues set in everyday life.

Emotionally, we were doing fairly well. Though the Akron house contract had fallen through and we had broken the lease on the Austin apartment, we were doing fine. There were some concerns about our partner in this ministry, but things were looking fine. We might say to friends, "Things are looking fine, and we have this great donation, so we're going to press ahead with the plans."

It was just a few days later that Jac wrote to me—again—about the church in Fullerton. He wrote a long and impassioned e-mail, asking me to "please just talk with the Senior Pastor." In getting that e-mail, I had an enormous "pause button" presented in my spiritual life. It wasn't a bad feeling or one of disappointment. It wasn't the thought of, "Boy, I messed up this time and God is correcting me." No, it was something different.

For many years, my view of God's will has been firmly based on the experiences of Nehemiah, in the biblical book that carries his name. Nehemiah was a civil servant who felt God's hand on him. While there are prophets in the Bible who speak for God and hear God's voice, Nehemiah had no such experiences. I have often compared Nehemiah to the prophet Jonah. Though Jonah heard God's direct command to go to a certain city, he disobeyed and went the other way. I like to call Jonah a "religious professional," which to my friends in ministry means a great deal since they, like I, are religious professionals.

It was Jonah, the religious professional, who clearly heard God's voice. It was Jonah who disobeyed and went the other way. It was Nehemiah, the bureaucrat for a mid-eastern king, who never heard God's voice. Nehemiah only received an "internal nudge" and acted on that.

With the second e-mail, I had to pause and wonder, "If God were going to give me an "internal nudge," how would He do it?" It was perfectly naturally and full of spiritual wisdom to not change our plans after the first e-mail. I really don't think that God wants us to jump at every opportunity that lands on our computer. But, I did have to wonder, "How would God get my attention?"

Though all things looked perfect for us to move out of church work and into full-time consulting and teaching, I wondered if God wasn't reshuffling the deck.

Some will wonder if we had just been overlooking common sense or plain facts in our plans. Perhaps we had "sinned" and so were missing "God's will." I don't think that this was the case. *I think that God was providing us with not just one but two wonderful options for the next phase of our lives.* God gave us some great plans and then presented us with some amazing plans.

I wrote back to Jac that I would be open to a conversation. I outlined the recent "bumps" of the Akron house falling out of contract and our breaking the lease of the apartment in Austin. While I didn't see that these were necessarily "game changers," we did want to explore what God might be doing. How else would God have gotten my attention ... and I really didn't want Him to take "extreme measures" to get my attention ... sickness, death of someone close, financial calamity. *Okay God, I will listen to You in some e-mails to see if You are redirecting our plans.*

Tami and I decided to drive to Dallas, escaping the winter weather of Ohio. Along that drive, the pastor from Fullerton phoned us. We had a long talk—what else is there to do in a car? I promised him that Tami and I would talk about his offer all afternoon—again, what else is there to do in a car? We were trapped in a drive from Memphis to Little Rock to Texarkana. All we could do was talk, think and pray!

Mike was the new Senior Pastor at EvFree Fullerton. It was a historic church that had gone through a few years of challenging transition. When Mike had been voted in as Senior Pastor, he immediately began to look for an Executive Pastor. In seeking advice with a number of people, he heard "talk to David Fletcher." By the end of a few months, he was sick of hearing my name. As he then had undertaken a search for an XP, he didn't find the person he was looking for. Finally, he decided to "talk to David Fletcher."

Walking Toward the Crisis

After that first long phone call with Mike, Tami and I talked and prayed. We thought about what God was doing and wondered if

He was redirecting our good plans. Why would God have us leave $225,000 on the table, unused? We didn't have an answer to that. In a very real way, it was a leadership crisis of positive proportions.

How do you determine if God wants you to walk away from some great things? Those things might be as positive as a great donation, a great opportunity or a great new phase of life. How do you determine what to do? That is when you encounter a crisis of positive proportions.

We reasoned and prayed that the way to move through this positive crisis was to walk towards it. If God wasn't in us going to Fullerton, then He would somehow show us that. We had to discover if Fullerton was like Newport Beach, just 20 miles away, flaunting their money and status. Was this the culture of Fullerton? Was God calling us to that? We hoped not.

God got our attention with a "little nudge." That was enough for us to pause and have some conversations, to review our plans and consider changes. The next step by God was more than a "little nudge." God radically redirected our lives through prayer.

It was the Sunday of the big week of discussions with the leaders at the church in Fullerton. The day before we had seen a townhome that would be good to rent. Yet, the owners lived in Korea and who knew how long it would take for us to find out if we could rent the place. On Sunday night, we asked God for four things for the week. We said, God this would be a great week if:

- We would hear on Monday that we could rent the townhouse. I could realize a dream by walking to work and we could easily entertain many guests.

- God would give us a positive time on Tuesday with the staff during the day and the Elders at night.

- At first, we didn't have a request for Wednesday. But, as long as we were asking, we asked that God would provide a buyer for our Akron house on Wednesday. It had gone into contract twice and fallen out twice! The realtor had not contacted us in a while and we had no idea if anyone was serious about the property.

- For Thursday, would God be so good as to give us a great time with the General Board of the Fullerton church.

With family and friends, we shared those very precise "requests." As God was in this crisis of positive proportions, we seemingly asked that He move from "a nudge" to a "clear statement." We needed God's affirmation to make this radical change in our plans.

On Monday, though the owners were in Korea and separated from us by many time zones, we heard that we could rent the townhouse. Their agent wrote: "Congratulation!!! (sic) They chose you as tenants. What term do you want, 1 or 2 year term?" In Orange County, where many houses are quickly rented and have multiple people vying for them, this was wonderful! The owners must have been e-mailing with their agent all during the night!

Tuesday was a long day. We had a great meeting with the staff in the morning and afternoon. That night we met with the Elders. It was a unanimous vote by the Elders that we come to Fullerton. They would pass on their recommendation to the General Board on Thursday.

As we met with more people on Wednesday, I checked my e-mail at a break. We had received a note from our real estate agent in Akron. I didn't have to open it. Though we hadn't talked to him in three weeks, just seeing his name told me that it was a contract. I turned off my phone for a few minutes. Why look at what I already knew to be a fact? After some time, I turned the phone back on and read the subject line: "Offer on 3061 Heron." We were in a meeting and I handed my phone to Tami—all we could do was give a smile to each other. The timing by God was too amazing. As an "afterword," let me include here, that this contract did go through and the house sold about thirty days later. God had let the other two contracts fall through. Over a period of five months, He let those contracts dissolve so that He could deliver one in our week in Fullerton, on the very day of our asking.

Tami and I didn't share these things with anyone. We wanted

to see how all four days rolled out.

Thursday came and we had a tremendous time with the General Board. We shared with them about our lives and left the room. The board then voted. Reentering the room, there was loud applause and we knew their decision. As I accepted their call to ministry at Fullerton, I recounted the four prayer requests for that week. For the first time, we shared how God had confirmed His direction in the answered prayers. Four days—four requests—four specific answers. God coordinated events in Fullerton, Akron and Korea. How could we say "no" to this crisis of positive proportions?

Thus, we came to realize that God was calling us to Fullerton. He was calling us to leave $225,000 on the table and not use those funds. Though the expansion of the work in East Asia was vital, it would have to be left for someone else at the present or later for our involvement. Those were shocking things for me. I don't think that I had ever left money on the table, and certainly not of that magnitude.

Lessons Learned

One of the core lessons that I learned was that money can be a good indicator for life and ministry plans. Many great decisions can be based on solid finances. However, money is not the best indicator of what I should do. Just because God has provided the funds for great ministry doesn't mean that I am supposed to do that work.

The American church, set in a culture of great materialism, points toward the phrase, "If the money comes in, then God must be in it." *I would put forward that this idea is patently false.* In a crisis of terrible proportions or positive proportions, money is not the key factor. The spiritual dynamic is the highest importance. Jesus had His earthly ministry without a home or bank account. Wealthy women supported Jesus and His disciples. Barnabas, in the book of Acts, had enough money to sell one of his fields to feed the poor. I need to be content with little money or surplus funds. The first lesson in a crisis of positive proportions is that *God is not necessarily saying "yes" just because there is sufficient money for a project.*

The second lesson is about *considering options.* A crisis of positive proportions is one where there are many good options to consider. In a crisis of terrible proportions, survival is based on solving problems with a high moral character. In a crisis of positive proportions, one must sort through many good things. There are multiple layers of positive things. What is the best thing to do in the current moment? What should be delayed or deferred? I must find the thing that God wants me to do right now. Though I had great opportunities in the U.S. and internationally to do consulting and teaching work, I had to sort out God's plan. *A crisis of positive proportions is about having too many great options—that is the crisis.* It is not a crisis of lack but a crisis of fullness.

I have long loved the words of my favorite Rabbi—Jesus—when He says in Luke 6:38:

"Give, and it will be given to you. A good measure, pressed down, shaken together and running over, will be poured into your lap. For with the measure you use, it will be measured to you."

I had never thought that God would have multiple ministry opportunities "running over" in my life. Oh, me of little faith. It is what the Rabbi said! The crisis is what to do with all those opportunities. *The second lesson is that a crisis of positive proportions brings too many wonderful options.*

The third lesson learned pertains to faithful friends. A crisis of positive proportions requires friends who will give advice, understanding that God may trump their advice. My friend Nathan gave superb advice about moving from a pastoral role to a consultant role. Our friends in Dallas not only offered $225,000 over three years, but began toward that goal by giving $53,000.

In the entire process, they firmly knew that God was doing something wonderful. I had to have frank conversations with them about their gift. Would a change in direction cause our friendship to be broken? Would they be greatly disheartened that the direction was changed? That dreary night in February held a vital conversation for us as we addressed this issue.

They proved to be friends who invested in a ministry but saw that God was bigger than their enormous donation. We all saw the opportunities to train people internationally but God said, "Not right now." *The third lesson is that a crisis of positive proportions brings to light friends who understand that God may trump their advice.*

The fourth and final lesson is one from the book of Proverbs.

We need to be strategic in our plans but must allow for God to guide us. In Proverbs 16:9 it says:

> "In their hearts humans plan their course, but the LORD establishes their steps."

God expects us to plan our course. We need to be thinking and making strategic plans for our lives. God, however, can invade our life and determine our next steps. I must put aside my "great plans" and allow Him to guide what I am to do. *The fourth lesson is that a crisis of positive proportions requires nimbleness to see when God is guiding our steps.*

There are seasons in our lives when we encounter a crisis of terrible proportions. There are also times when we find ourselves in a crisis of positive proportions. God floods our lives with positive options, like that "good measure pressed down and overflowing." We can hardly know what to do because the options are so wonderful. The crisis of positive proportions requires a nimbleness of spirit to see God at work.

AND NOW IT'S YOUR TURN
D. Scott Barfoot, David R. Fletcher

Everyman & Everywoman

Each person has a unique story of how God is working in his or her life. To help us all grow, Scott and I brought together the articles of this book. The authors have stories to share from the richness of their lives and the depth of their spiritual intimacy with God. None of the writers are famous. None are well published. None have reached the finish line in their journey. In this sense, all the authors have an *everyman's* or *everywoman's* story. Thus, this book is really about you.

This book is what your story is and what your story could be. It can inspire you in a crisis of terrible proportions. It can encourage you in a crisis of positive proportions.

This book is a collection of articles on *Crisis Leadership*. There has been transparency and authenticity in the stories.

Justin Beadles shared about the crisis of how to leave his position as senior pastor, even in the midst of a thriving church ministry. The enormous marital challenge of being served divorce papers while in ministry was spoken to from Tim Crow's life. Rod MacIlvaine showed that a leadership crisis is not a time to just react and solve problems, but a time to submit to the discipline of learning.

There were multi-national lessons to be learned from Manila in Stephen Tan's global insights. He focused on how to bring radical change to a conservative church culture. Suzanne Martinez addressed dealing with crisis when under fire in the high-pressure atmosphere of the military. Ray Chang presented an issue with hiring staff and the key lessons learned in this process.

Caleb Kaltenbach wrote about the stagnation and then

growth in the church where he served as a new senior pastor. Scott Barfoot addressed how to create a culture of trust that thrives in a climate of crisis. David Fletcher's article addressed the surplus of positive ministry options that God can bring in a crisis of positive proportions.

Your Story

A huge disservice that you can do is to muddle through a crisis. To plod through a crisis, letting the situation determine how the events roll out, is missing the opportunity. My (Scott) great-aunt Ilene always says, "Scotty, walk through the valleys, don't wallow in them." A crisis is a time to keep your heart soft and your chin up. It is a "for such a time as this" Esther-like moment, to deepen your trust in the Lord and to harness your leadership gifts in a way you never imagined. A working mother with a sick child and a work deadline has the opportunity to rise to the challenge and change the world.

A second disservice that you can do is to solve a crisis without learning God's lessons in it. I (David) remember Dr. Horace Woods, a medical doctor in Dallas. In his nineties, he had a heart attack and was taken to the hospital. Some young nurse was trying to be nice. Peering down at him on the gurney, she said, "Don't worry Dr. Woods, you will be fine." Not content with this comment, Dr. Woods replied, "I'm not worried, because I know where I am going when I die. What about you?"

Most of us journey to the hospital with one thing in mind: *fix the problem, now!* In those crises, God is certainly not opposed to that prayer. Yet, He also has something much greater in view. God wants people to see Him at work!

Share Your Story

This is an everyman's and everywoman's book. On our XP-Press website (www.XPPress.org) we have provided a place for you to post your *Crisis Leadership* story. We would love to hear from you. How has God worked through you in a time of crisis? How have you, as a mom or a dad, a leader or a follower, the top-dog or the worker-bee, responded to a crisis?

ABOUT THE AUTHORS

Dr. D. Scott Barfoot

Scott serves as Director of Dallas Theological Seminary's Doctor of Ministry program. He received a Master of Theology in Pastoral Ministries from Dallas Theological Seminary, and a Doctor of Philosophy in Organizational Leadership from Regent University. Scott aspires to equip and empower global executive, pastoral, and educational ministry leaders who impact the next generation for the cause of Christ. He is married to Debbie and they have three children.

Pastor Justin Beadles

Justin currently serves as the Pastor of Countryside Baptist Church in Stillwater, Oklahoma—the very church where he first learned grace. He was reared on a family farm and received his undergraduate degree in Agriculture from Oklahoma State University. After graduating from Dallas Theological Seminary in 2000, Justin served as the Pastor of Grace Bible Church in Nacogdoches, Texas for eleven years. He and his wife, Heather, have three sons and one daughter.

Dr. Raymond Y. Chang

Ray has been the pastor of Ambassador Church in Brea, California for the past ten years. He went to Talbot and Dallas Theological Seminary, earning a Masters in Divinity and a Masters in Sacred Theology; he received his Doctorate in Ministry at Trinity Divinity Evangelical School. Ray has extensive ministry experience in second generation Korean American and multiethnic ministry. He is married to Sun Joo Chang and has twin daughters.

Dr. Tim Crow

Tim currently serves as the pastor at Firestone Park Baptist Church in Akron, Ohio and teaches courses in Old Testament and Hebrew at Ashland Theological Seminary. He received his Masters of Theology in Old Testament and Hebrew from Dallas Theological Seminary and his Doctor of Philosophy in Ancient Near-Eastern Studies at the University of Liverpool's School of Classics, Archaeology, and Oriental Studies. Tim and his wife, Leslie, have four children.

Dr. David R. Fletcher

David is best described as a spiritual entrepreneur. He has been a pastor for over thirty years and now serves as the Executive Pastor at EvFree Fullerton. David founded XPastor, a global ministry tool to churches of all sizes. He has taught at Dallas Theological Seminary and founded the Doctor of Ministries program at ETS India. David created People Patterns®, both the online indicator and the book. He is married to Tami and they have two grown children.

Pastor Caleb Kaltenbach

Caleb has served in various senior and associate pastor roles in churches in Southern California and Texas since 1999. Additionally, Caleb teaches at Dallas Christian College and is a member of the college's Board of Trustees. Caleb is a graduate of Ozark Christian College, holds a Masters of Biblical and Theological Studies from Talbot School of Theology and is working on his Doctor of Ministry in Preaching and Leadership at Dallas Theological Seminary. He is married to Amy and they have two children.

Dr. W. Rodman MacIlvaine III

Rod MacIlvaine is the founding senior pastor of Grace Community Church in Bartlesville, Oklahoma. He serves as a Fellow with the Veritas Center for Faith, Freedom and Justice at Oklahoma Wesleyan University and is an adjunct professor in the Doctor of Ministry Department at Dallas Theological Seminary. For the past ten years he has worked to multiply church planters in the Spanish-speaking Caribbean through coaching and training. He and his wife have four children and six grandchildren.

Dr. Suzanne Martinez

Through her past experiences in corporate, government and church contexts, God has given Suzanne a passion to help churches develop healthy leadership and cultures that maximize people's contributions to His kingdom. Suzanne earned her Masters degrees from Trinity Evangelical Divinity School and Capital Bible Seminary and her Doctor of Ministry degree from Dallas Theological Seminary. Suzanne lives near Washington, DC, with her husband and their two children.

Pastor Stephen G. Tan

Stephen is the Senior Pastor of Grace Christian Church of the Philippines. He graduated summa cum laude from Dallas Theological Seminary with a Master of Theology and was given the J. Dwight Pentecost Award in Bible Exposition. He has spoken at conferences and churches throughout North America and Asia. Stephen previously worked as a management consultant for Deloitte and Touche USA. He is married to Cindy and they have three children.